A Young Scientist's Guide to FAULTY FREAKS of NATURE

A Young Scientist's Guide

to FAULTY FREAKS

of NATURE

GIBBS SMITH
TO ENRICH AND INSPIRE HUMANKIND

INCLUDING **20** EXPERIMENTS for the sink, bathtub and backyard

JAMES DOYLE

Illustrations by ANDREW BROZYNA

Manufactured in China in January 2013 by Toppan

First Edition
17 16 15 14 13 .... 5 4 3 2 1

This book contains activities that may carry an element of risk or danger. Readers of the
book are urged to make wise decisions and to consult prudent adults before engaging
in activities. The author and publisher disclaim all responsibility for injury resulting
from the performance of any activities described in this book. Readers assume all legal
responsibility for their actions.

Published by
Gibbs Smith
P.O. Box 667
Layton, Utah 84041

1.800.835.4993 orders
www.gibbs-smith.com

Designed and illustrated by Andrew J. Brozyna
Gibbs Smith books are printed on either recycled, 100% post-consumer waste, FSC-
certified papers or on paper produced from sustainable PEFC-certified forest/controlled
wood source. Learn more at www.pefc.org.

Library of Congress Cataloging-in-Publication Data

Doyle, James, 1972–
  A young scientist's guide to faulty freaks of nature : including 20 experiments for the sink,
bathtub and backyard / James Doyle ; illustrations by Andrew Brozyna. — 1st ed.
    p. cm.
  ISBN 978-1-4236-2455-4
1. Nature—Effect of human beings on—Juvenile literature. 2. Science—Miscellanea—
Juvenile literature. I. Brozyna, Andrew, ill. II. Title.
  GF75.D69 2013
  304.2—dc23
                              2012037728

For Oonágh

Contents

Back Away From the Book!

"I repeat! ... Back Away From the Book!" The contents of this book are not suitable for you and your "kind." You are, after all, very likely to be a member of a group of species that now numbers more than seven billion creatures. A group often referred to as "humans," "Homo sapiens" and even, "Earthlings." Despite your kind being clever, curious, inventive and at top of the food chain, you have managed to make some seriously monumental mistakes and mind-boggling mishaps.

You guys have single-handedly messed up the planet with a combination of completely, crazy chemistry, birdbrained biology and foolhardy physics. Some of your top scientists have been seriously suspect, and they can take the credit for creating planetary-wide chaos. In your hand you have the true story of the little bird that sounds like a chainsaw when it sings, the food that can make your face fall off, the experiment that made an entire sea vanish and much, much more!

If you are ready to learn from the silly mistakes of the past, then this is the book for you. This book is your guide to some of the strangest science ever seen and you'll also discover that some of the things scientists told you were wrong ... were actually right! You'll find that the fictional Hobbit was indeed fact. You'll see how the fantasy books of Harry Potter have influenced the world of science forever, and you'll meet an all-new creature called "spider goat." So, if you have a thirst for the weird, the wonderful and the downright wacky then this is the science book for you. This is *A Young Scientist's Guide to Faulty Freaks of Nature*.

Fascinating and Fearful Discoveries

Humans Have a Habit of Mistaking Hobbits

Scientists are supposed to be among the smartest humans on Earth. After all, they invent amazing things, they find cures for terrible diseases and they know very clever stuff. As a result, most people wouldn't expect them to get things wrong but even the smartest of humans can get things pretty messed up.

Take the idea of hobbits for example. Humans first discovered these tiny, fictional creatures from middle-earth in J. R. R. Tolkien's stories, which include *The Lord of the Rings* trilogy. Tolkien describes hobbits as "relatives" of the human race but points out that they are a separate "branch" of human beings. In his books, he writes about the similarities and differences between humans and hobbits by describing them as "Big People" and "Little People." The world of science paid little attention to Tolkien's writings and scientists were quite happy for them to appear as fantasy in books and movies to entertain people's imaginations.

Until just over 10 years ago, scientists believed that Homo sapiens (us) were the only human species on Earth since our cousins, the Neanderthals died out some 30,000 years ago. That was until 2001 when the tiny "hobbits" of Southeast Asia were discovered—blowing apart the belief held by the scientific world—that hobbits didn't exist.

The discovery of the three-foot (1 m) tall skeleton was made in a cave in 2001 by a team of Australian and Indonesian scientists on the Indonesian island of Flores. Hence, the name "The Flores Hobbit" and the scientific name *"Homo floresiensis."* At first, the scientists believed that they had found the skeleton of a small child but following detailed tests, it was confirmed that the tiny specimen was, in fact, a full-grown adult. This tiny species would have stood about the height of a three-year-old child when fully grown. Their small stature is thought to have been caused by island dwarfism—where a group is cut off from the outside world and has only a very limited food supply, which, in turn, greatly restricts growth. Ironically, the tales of Bilbo Baggins and Frodo may not be as far fetched as we might first think.

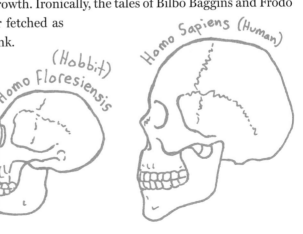

TRIVIA *The Hobbit* was first published in 1937 by J. R. R. Tolkien and has sold over 100 million copies to date. The success of the book resulted three Hobbit movies. For fun, facts, trailers and downloads about *The Hobbit* 2012, 2013 and 2014 movies go to the website: www.thehobbit.com.

YOUNG SCIENTIST ACTIVITY
How to make a Stalactite

Hobbits aren't the only cool things you can find in a deep cave. Some of them are filled with magical shapes and objects created by the processes of nature. With this activity, you can build your very own stalactite. Stalactites form in limestone caves as water packed with minerals seeps through the ground over thousands of years to form amazing icicle-like shapes.

EQUIPMENT NEEDED:

Two paperclips

One length of wool

Two empty jam jars

Epsom salt

One spoon

One saucer or small dish

INSTRUCTIONS:

1. Take your two jars and fill them with really hot (but not boiling) water.

2. Now take your spoon and start adding the Epsom salt to both jars. Keep doing this, stirring the jars until all Epsom salts have dissolved.

3. Place a saucer or small dish in between both jars. Take the wool and cut

a piece long enough to reach the bottom of each jar and bridge the gap between the jars.

4. Now tie the paperclips to each end of the wool to create a weight and lower the ends into their respective jars.

5. Simply leave for 3 or 4 days and see what happens.

Science Factoid

Capillary action, which is the upward movement of water, helps the water move out of each jar along the piece of wool. As the solution moves along the wool from both jars, eventually the two solutions meet and begin to form drips downward. The water in the solution starts to evaporate and leaves behind a solid-growing stalactite.

Lyre the Liar

The lyrebird is an extraordinary creature with a very special talent. Native to the rain forests of Australia, this shy and often hidden bird is a master of disguise. You see, the lyrebird loves to sing and will quite happily belt out its songs for most of the daylight hours, but the lyrebird's talent lies in its ability to "lie" or at least "trick" other animals.

Lyrebirds can, very convincingly, copy the individual songs of other birds and the noise created by flocks of birds. Even better, they can also copy the calls of other animals, including those of koala bears and the howls of wild dingoes.

HUMAN IMPACT

In its rain forest environment, the lyrebird is very happy to sing and trick those who live alongside it. But, unfortunately, humans have destroyed much of the lyrebird's habitat. Our desire for more and more rain forest materials has meant that the lyrebirds are coming into contact with increasing numbers of human beings, and this has added an unbelievable twist to the lyrebird's ability to copy other sounds.

Scientists and researchers have now recorded the lyrebird copying the noises they hear from the loggers and their equipment. These include the perfect mimicking of the buzz of chainsaws as the trees of the rain forest are cut away, the rumble of a car engine or the sirens of a car alarm. Better still, the little "liars" can even copy the sound of gunshots, camera shutters, baby cries and dogs barking.

ANCIENT LYRE

IF YOU GO DOWN TO THE WOODS TODAY . . .

So, if you find yourself in the Australian rain forest, don't get frightened or paranoid by the noises that surround you. The sound of gunshots and dogs may not mean that you are being hunted down. The high-pitched screams of a baby crying far from any other humans doesn't necessarily mean that you have entered a horror movie. You may have just encountered the little "liar," the lyrebird.

LYRE BIRD

TRIVIA Watch a clip of the magic mimic at work in the Australian rain forest as he produces camera shutter sounds, car alarms and chainsaws by following this link: video.nationalgeographic.com/video/animals/birds-animals/ground-birds/weirdest-superb-lyrebird.

YOUNG SCIENTIST ACTIVITY
The Sounds of Glass

It's not just the little lyrebird that can make weird and wonderful sounds. This activity will show that even ordinary drinking glasses can be used to make musical sounds.

EQUIPMENT NEEDED:

Six to eight drinking glasses
(Ideally, they will all be the same size)

Water

One jug

One pencil or a small wooden stick

INSTRUCTIONS:

1. Take your group of glasses and line them up in a row.

2. Now take the jug and fill it with water. Then take the jug and pour a small amount of water into the first glass. As you move through the glasses, add a little more water to each one so that the last glass has the most and is practically full.

3. Lift the pencil or wooden stick and hit the glass with the largest amount of water in it and listen to the sound the glass makes. Repeat the process with

the glass with the smallest amount in it and listen and see if the sound it makes is different.

4. Now try with all the glasses and see if you can compose a piece of music.

Science Factoid

All of the glasses make a different sound when hit with the pencil or stick. The glass holding the largest amount of water has the lowest tone and the glass with the smallest amount of water will have the highest tone. These sounds are caused by the tiny vibrations that are made when your pencil/stick hits the glass. The strike makes sound waves that travel through the water. A larger volume of water means the waves have farther to travel, which means slower vibrations and a deeper tone. The glass with the least amount of water has faster vibrations and a higher-pitched tone.

The Harry Potter Dinosaur

Dinosaurs are normally named after the scientists who discover them, where they were found or for a special feature, such as a long tail or large claws. The *Dracorex hogwartsia* has made scientific history as the first dinosaur species to be named after a fictitious (made-up) place from the tales of the schoolboy wizard, Harry Potter.

The first part of the name, "Dracorex," comes from two Latin words meaning dragon (draco) and king (rex). Add the "Hogwartsia" bit (after the Hogwarts School of Witchcraft and Wizardry) and you have the grandly titled "Dragon King of Hogwarts." The dinosaur is a member of the pachycephalosaur family. But it is unique for having both a flat forehead and a series of lumps, bumps and horns that have never been seen before. Most dinosaurs in this family grouping have domed foreheads.

The dinosaur was first discovered by three friends from Iowa in 2004. They stumbled across it on a fossil-collecting trip to the Hell Creek Formation in South Dakota. They then donated it to the Children's Museum of Indianapolis where one of the museum's scientists, Victor Porter, took more than two years to piece the fragments of its skull together before confirming that it was a newly discovered species. The 66-million-year-old dinosaur fossil was then formally named by Porter and fellow scientist Bob Bakker after the fictional Hogwarts Academy from the popular Harry Potter books. They felt that the unique appearance of the specimen was similar to the dragons, griffins and mythical creatures described in J. K. Rowling's books.

In fact, the museum's president and CEO Dr. Jeffrey H. Patchen stated: "What a fantastic opportunity to merge real science with J. K. Rowling's marvelous gift of storytelling."

SCIENCE OR FICTION?

Some scientists feel that Dr. Patchen's comments are a real threat to the world of science which is based on facts, evidence and detailed research. They say that the naming of a real dinosaur after a place that doesn't exist makes a mockery of real science. Worse still, some scientists believe the skull may not be evidence of a completely new species at all but may simply be from a young pachycephalosaurus. They argue that it is possible for juveniles to be born with flat skulls and that the prominent pachycephalosaurus dome can begin to appear as the animal grows into adulthood.

For the time being, this theory remains unproven, but there is no question that the skull is a real dinosaur skull and that "The Dragon King of Hogwarts" will continue to weave its magic on the world of science for some time to come.

TRIVIA

- When *Harry Potter and the Prisoner of Azkaban* was released in the U.K., the publisher asked bookstores not to sell the book until schools were closed for the day to prevent fans from skipping school to get a copy.

- It might appear an incredible coincidence but Harry Potter and J. K. Rowling share the same birthday, July 31st.

- Hogwarts School's Latin motto *"Draco Domiens Nunquam Titillandus"* translates into English as "never tickle a sleeping dragon."

- King's Cross train station in London has become so popular with Harry Potter fans wanting to take pictures of platform 9 and 10 that management at the station have erected a sign that reads "platform 9 and three-quarters."

- For games, quizzes and training in magic, log on to www. pottermore.com.

YOUNG SCIENTIST ACTIVITY
Magic Mirror

Harry Potter and his wizarding friends aren't the only people who can wield magic. This very simple experiment uses clever science to make you vanish into thin air.

EQUIPMENT NEEDED:

One large flat area to work

One person (you to start with)

One pair of scissors

A foot long (30 cm) length of aluminium foil

INSTRUCTIONS:

1. Take the roll of aluminium foil and roll it out over a flat area.

2. Using your judgment, estimate a length of foil around 1 foot long (30 cm). Take the scissors and cut the foil from the roll.

3. Hold your piece of foil up in the air in front of you. Turn it to inspect both sides. You will notice that one side of the foil is shinier than the other. Place your piece of foil shiny side up.

4. Kneel down over your piece of foil and you'll be able to see your reflection. Now lift the foil and gently scrunch it up in your hands but not too much or you'll need to start all over again.

5. Place the piece of foil back on the ground and flatten it out a little so that it looks fairly flat but still has tiny bumps (just as a scrunched piece of paper might look after it has been flattened out again).

6. Kneel down over your piece of foil again ... what happened?

Science Factoid

On the flat, smooth piece of foil, light rays bounce off the surface in a perfectly straight line, allowing you to see your image in exactly the same way a mirror would. The crumpled piece of foil, however, is a whole mass of uneven lumps and bumps. This causes the light rays to bounce around in many different directions and prevents your mirror image from forming. Try this magic mirror on friends to show them how wicked of a wizard you really are.

Fantastic Fears

Most human beings have a fear of something or other. We all know someone with a fear of heights or a fear of spiders or snakes, but science has also listed and studied some human fears that you probably haven't ever heard of before. Scientists all over the world have gone to the trouble of naming human fears of pretty much everything. They do this by choosing a very big word and adding the word "phobia" at the end. This makes even the simplest fear sound highly technical. Just take a look at the table below to see some little-known phobias and if you want a few days off school, you need to tell mom that you have didaskaleinophobia—which is science-speak for the fear of going to school.

PHOBIA	WHAT IT IS
Lachanophobia	This is the fear of vegetables
Vestiphobia	This is the fear of clothes
Cyberphobia	The fear of computers
Ablutophobia	The fear of bathing and washing
Chronomentrophobia	The fear of clocks
Didaskaleinophobia	This is the fear of school
Genuphobia	The fear of knees
Hippopotomonstrosesquippedaliophobia	Is a very long word which means you have a fear of long words
Linonophobia	This is the fear of string or thread
Peladophobia	The fear of bald people
Sciophobia	This is the fear of shadows
Nomophobia	The fear of losing mobile phone contact

TRIVIA Despite the fact that humans have a long list of fears relating to going outside, research by the Royal Society for the Prevention of Accidents (RoSPA) in the U.K. shows that many of our worst fears are encountered much closer to home. Believe it or not, accidents happening in and around the home are caused by the simplest and least threatening items you might find.

In conducting research into one year's worth of accidents, RoSPA found that twigs and branches had caused over 8,000 accidents that year. Almost 8,500 accidents had resulted from incidents with trousers. Almost 9,000 difficulties were caused by Q-tips, while nearly 10,500 involved humans having trouble with cardboard boxes and more than 70,000 accidents involved ordinary training shoes.

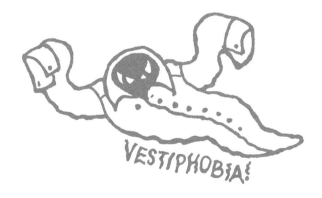

VESTIPHOBIA!

Silly Science-Speak

The scientists of the world have done an excellent job of making themselves appear rather clever. One way of doing this is to use large words to describe everyday things. That way, most of us ordinary citizens don't know what they are talking about and we simply believe that they are dealing with really scientific stuff. You'd be amazed at some of the silly and strange things that some scientists study. If I told you I was a specialist in the fields of emetology and garbology, you'd probably be impressed . . . until you discovered what they really involve.

The facing table gives just a flavor of silly science-speak in action and what it translates to in ordinary, everyday human-speak:

SCIENTIFIC FIELD	WHAT IT IS
Brontology	The scientific study of thunder
Conchology	The study of shells
Cryptozoology	The study of animals whose existence cannot yet be proved
Dendrochronology	The study of tree rings
Emetology	The study of vomiting
Garbology	The study of garbage
Oikology	The study of housekeeping
Oology	The study of eggs
Osmics	The scientific study of smells
Phrenology	The study of the bumps on your head
Telmatology	The study of swamps
Urenology	The study of rust molds
Xylology	The study of wood

Food That Will Make Your Face Fall off and Other Delightful Dishes

Okay . . . Okay, we know at this point that humans can make seriously silly mistakes and get things badly wrong, but some of these mistakes can result in extremely unpleasant side effects and even death. In this chapter, we will focus on some of the gross and downright deadly foods people eat.

#1. POLAR BEAR LIVER

The idea of eating any kind of liver at all probably makes you want to throw up before you've even started, but you'd be amazed at how many people enjoy different varieties of the stuff. In some South American countries, deep-fried chicken livers are a delicacy, and in Japan (if you can stomach it) you can enjoy sashimi, which contains raw fish liver. However, there is one liver that tops them all—polar bear liver is a meal you're never likely to forget!

At the home of the polar bear, the Arctic, the native peoples have a long history of feasting on our furry friend but they are fully aware of the dangers associated with eating its liver. No problem there then, until the arrival of the polar explorers who, unfortunately, tucked into a liver or two.

The effects on the explorers depended on just how much liver they had eaten. The typical symptoms include vomiting, headaches and aching joints, but the most disgusting side effect of dining on polar bear liver is a process called "desquamation," which can result in your skin falling off. If you have only eaten a small amount, you may be lucky and only experience some flaking around your mouth and face, but there are detailed accounts of full-body skin loss, coma and even death for those who have eaten too much. This painful experience is caused because the polar bear liver is jam-packed with vitamin A and eating too much in a short period of time results in acute hypervitaminosis A. So, if you are offered polar bear liver . . . beware!

#2. FUGU

The fugu fish can kill you within a matter of hours if it is not properly prepared. This requires a highly skilled, expert chef to remove the liver and reproductive organs of the fish. Only fugu-authorized chefs are legally allowed to serve the fish. These guys have been trained for up to three years to do the job.

If you are served a badly prepared fugu, watch out! It contains a poison known as tetrodotoxin, which will paralyze your muscles and lead to suffocation. I should tell you at this point that there is no antidote for fugu poisoning; however, you may survive with the help of a respirator until the poison starts to wear off. Experts say that if you make it through the first 24 hours of the event, you could just live to see another day.

#3. CASU MARZU

At first glance, this is simply Italian sheep's-milk cheese from Sardinia. Some cheese experts compare how it tastes to the more famous gorgonzola. A closer look will let you see that your cheese is actually moving ... with wriggling maggots ... UURRGH!!!

You see, part of the early cheese-making process requires flies to land and hatch their eggs on the cheese. The digestive juices of the fly larvae start off the cheese-making. On public health grounds, the European Union has banned this cheese. However, despite being illegal, some say you can still buy casu marzu from the shepherds of Sardinia. Supporters of the wriggling goo say the cheese is fine as long as it's still "wriggling," and that it is only dangerous if the maggots are dead. When eaten alive, they actually survive the trip through your stomach before exiting on the other side . . . nice!

#4. SANNAKJI AKA
WRIGGLING OCTOPUS

Once these little guys are in your stomach, you're safe, but it's getting them there that's the tricky bit. This dish is traditionally served in Korean restaurants and requires the removal of the octopus' legs while it's still alive.

This means tentacles are wriggling and moving around on your plate. The danger for you is that the little suction cups on the tentacles stick inside your mouth and throat, causing choking. It is estimated that in South Korea, around six people a year die from eating this dish. If you are going to try it, make sure you chew it well and wash it down with lots of liquids (or should that be *li-squids!*).

TRIVIA A FEW OTHERS TO WATCH OUT FOR ON THE DINNER TABLE

- Penguin eggs are perfectly edible and will bring you no harm, but the sight of a cooked penguin egg is enough to put you off your breakfast for good with a red-orange yolk and blue-grey "white"— not really what you'd call an "EGGS-ELLENT EGGS-PERIENCE."

- Cassava is a vegetable central to the African diet. When prepared properly, it is harmless. If not, a single kilo of the stuff contains enough cyanide to kill four adults.

- The giant bullfrog. The bullfrog is classed as a delicacy in Namibia, Africa. The Namibians eat the entire giant bullfrog except for its internal organs. In many cultures, certain parts of the frog such as the legs are eaten as most frogs have poisonous skin and poisonous internal organs. A premature bullfrog is said to contain a certain toxin, which could lead to kidney failure in those who eat it.

- Chocolate. Yes! chocolate because it contains an alkaloid called "theobromine," which in very high doses can be toxic to humans. The bigger risk is caused to species such as dogs, which can be killed by eating much smaller amounts.

YOUNG SCIENTIST ACTIVITY
Make Your Own Fizzy Drinks

This activity will help you create cool, refreshing and fizzy lemonade that (unlike the foods just mentioned) will actually be a pleasant experience.

EQUIPMENT NEEDED:

One six-ounce drinking glass

1 1/2 to 2 tablespoons lemon juice

1/2 cup cold water

1 teaspoon of baking soda

1 1/2 to 2 tablespoons sugar
(to add as sweetener)

INSTRUCTIONS:

1. Pour lemon juice in glass.

2. Add water.

3. Add one teaspoon of baking soda and stir in well.

4. Add sugar and taste. (Add more sugar if needed.)

Science Factoid

You should have just made a fizzy lemonade drink. The bubbles in the drink are caused by the baking soda being added to the lemon-water mixture. These bubbles are carbon dioxide gas and are exactly the same as the ones you'll find in store-bought fizzy drinks. The bubbles appear when the lemon, which is acidic, is added to the baking soda, which is a base or alkali. When the acid and base meet, a chemical reaction occurs that creates the fizzy bubbles.

Neanderthal: *Not a Dumb Brute After All*

For a very long time, scientists classed Neanderthal man as a dumb brute who was in many ways inferior to modern man. In fact, the term "Neanderthal" is used in everyday speech to describe a person as unintelligent, caveman-like or outdated, and it has even been used to describe someone who views females as lesser than males. Despite these widely held ideas, recent research shows that much of what we believe about Neanderthals is very wrong.

Neanderthal man is the human race's closest and best-known cousin. From early times we have painted them as ape-like, brutish monsters. Yes, from close-up the Neanderthal man appears different from us. He would typically have a pale skin color. His hair would probably be red. He would have a very dominant brow, a big jaw and a large nose. He would be physically larger than most humans with a more muscular build than most of today's athletes, but some scientists are convinced that he was not hugely different in appearance to us. They argue that a typical Neanderthal dressed in modern clothing would quite easily blend in to the surroundings of a modern city.

DNA SEIZES THE DAY

Only a few short years ago, the results from tests carried out by a Swedish genetic scientist, Svante Paabo, were published. He had successfully extracted DNA from Neanderthal remains. These tests, amazingly, showed that Neanderthals and humans from Europe and Asia may well have interbred, a process that makes our two species much closer than anyone had believed before. He also located a gene scientists call the "FOXP2" gene. It was found in a similar form to the one modern humans possess. The presence of such a gene suggests that Neanderthal man may have also been capable of using complex language like us.

THE CARING "MONSTER"

One final messed-up idea about Neanderthal man is the image that he was typically an uncaring, savage brute with little feeling. More recent evidence shows that Neanderthals were caring, loving and considerate to others. Likewise, many of us held the belief that Neanderthals were spear-throwing savages who fed only on meat, but again, as recently as 2010, scientists discovered plant remains in the teeth of Neanderthal individuals. They found peas, beans, grains and dates, a further piece of evidence that shows that our Neanderthal cousins were much more like us than earlier science led us to believe.

Humans Invented Extreme Sports

Really cool humans like surfers, white water rafters and bungee jumpers pride themselves on being different than the rest of us. They see themselves as people who push nature's boundaries and believe that they are at the cutting edge of the sports world.

Extreme sports people are quite pleased with themselves about inventing cool ways to play with planet Earth but they've got one basic thing mixed up—humans didn't invent these sports at all—nature got there first! You may not be able to imagine a spider hang-gliding or bungee jumping high into the upper atmosphere or beetles and other tiny insects "surfing" down rivers and across vast oceans. Not to mention the little snail that simply loves rafting. In this chapter you'll find out a little more about nature's epic adventurers.

NATURE'S OWN EXTREME SPORTS

The scientists who study spiders are called "arachnologists." For a very long time they were completely puzzled as to how spiders made it onto isolated and unpopulated islands in the center of our oceans, but eventually they discovered that most spider species have the ability to float through the high atmosphere of Earth using an amazing process known as "ballooning."

HOW TO BALLOON

For a spider who is an extreme sports enthusiast there a few highly technical steps in this daredevil procedure:

1. The spider needs to stand in an exposed area such as the edge of a leaf.

2. The spider then fires out a thread of silk from its abdomen, and it gets caught up in the moving air currents.

3. The spider then spins more and more silk creating a kite-like structure or parachute before releasing its surface grip and soaring skyward . . . YEEEE-HAAA!!

Scientists have proven that spiders can reach several miles (thousands of meters) in altitude in the atmosphere and have crossed more than 100 thousand miles (hundreds of kilometers) in distance using this cross between hang gliding and bungee jumping.

NATURE'S SURFERS

Another means of extreme transport for beetles, insects and even larger animals such as frogs and snakes is to surf along on logs, branches and whole trees down rivers and across oceans. Others, such as pseudo-scorpions are even more inventive and hitch a ride on the back of large winged insects by clamping on to the hairs on their backs to take flight.

TRIVIA UPSIDE DOWN RAFTING

The very clever Janthinidae snail uses the slime produced from its "foot" (the gooey bit that a snail uses to move across the ground) to form a "raft" of bubbles which keep it afloat at the top of the ocean—a bit like creating its own set of floats or air bags. The ingenious creature folds its foot around a pocket of air and then attaches the new air bubble to the rest of its raft of air bubbles before setting off for sail while lying upside down with its "air foot" or raft pointed upward.

YOUNG SCIENTIST ACTIVITY
Extreme Bucketing

This activity will help you find out about the forces all around you while combining it with the fun of spinning around with a bucket full of water. Be careful though, if not carried out correctly, you and others could get mighty wet.

EQUIPMENT NEEDED:

Outdoor space (if you get this wrong indoors, you could ruin a lot of things)

One plastic bucket

Water

INSTRUCTIONS:

1. Take the bucket and fill it to around halfway full.

2. Go outside and find a clear area where you can spin around without hitting into anyone or anything.

3. Take your now half-filled bucket by the handle and extend your arm straight out by your side at a 90-degree angle to the rest of your body. (As a check that you are doing this right—turn your head and place your chin on the shoulder of the arm that is holding the bucket. If your chin and arm are in line then you are all set.)

4. Now for the hard part—begin to spin your bucket upward toward the sky and then back down again toward the ground in a circular motion. This will take practice, but your aim is to spin the bucket fast enough to keep the water inside the bucket. If you succeed, you will have messed with centripetal force.

Science Factoid

You will probably think that this an extraordinary extreme sport—remember you need to put a half full bucket of water over your head, but science and forces are at work here to keep you dry. As the water and the bucket hit the right speed, centripetal force comes into play. This is the force that acts on any object that moves in a circular path. As a result, the water is directed toward the outside of the circle around which it is moving. This type of force keeps the water inside the bucket even when it is above your head—unless, of course, you slow down or stop suddenly—in which case you might need a towel.

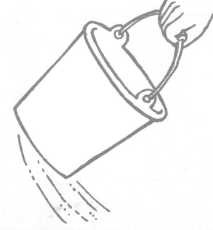

Catastrophic Chemicals

Messing with Evolution

Now, this one is a real mess and you definitely need to concentrate hard on the science involved. Imagine a world where humans have messed stuff up so badly that they have released so much female hormone into the water supply that it could be causing a dramatic change in the male gender and not just in humans—scientists believe they are witnessing biological changes in the animal world as well. Worse still, what's the future for a planet where every creature is a female?

WHAT'S HAPPENING?

All the while humans go about their daily business, they are often blissfully unaware of the damage they do. Scientists have discovered worryingly high levels of the hormone estrogen in the rivers and lakes of the world. Ordinarily, estrogen is fine. After all, it's what makes half of the human population female and is even found (in lower levels) in males as well, but it is the dramatic rise in hormone found in our water supplies that is beginning to worry the scientific world. Research has found that estrogen is being released into our environment from large industries like sewage treatment works (the scientific name for the cleansing of your poop!) and these "treatments" begin to build up in our water supplies.

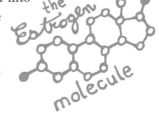

WORRYING SIGNS

Scientists are pointing out dramatic changes in animal and human evolution that could threaten many species on Earth. Specialists in Florida are warning of major changes in the bodies of male alligators. Others describe serious deformities in species such as otters, while there is an increasing number of male fish appearing that look just like female fish! Confused? You should be. Scientists argue that, if the rate of increase of estrogen levels in our water supplies continues, we will soon be looking at big changes for male humans.

WHAT YOU CAN EXPECT:

- Watch out for the thinning and then loss of your body hair.
- Watch how the tone of your voice rises to a higher pitch.
- Beware of the redistribution of your body fat to your hips, thighs and butt (in other words, you become more female shaped).

On the plus side, baldness among females is much rarer than it is for men. So, it could be the perfect cure for the old slap heads of the world, but you might also have a sudden interest in shoes and make-up. Either way, a species with only one gender isn't going to last very long.

Fatbergs: *Coming to a City Near You!*

Humans have all manner of ways to mess up this planet and just when you think you've seen them all, the human race comes up with a completely new way to cause havoc. As more and more humans move to live in cities, it means things get more and more crowded and more and more congested, but in our largest cities, called "megacities," there is a new problem. Fatbergs, named using a twist on the term icebergs, these babies can bring things to a standstill in a whole different way.

Fatbergs are the name that has been given to the sometimes huge blocks of congealed cooking oil mixed with wet wipes found in our sewer networks. As they solidify, they block the sewers that run beneath our largest cities, such as New York and Tokyo, but it's in London,

England, where there are real problems. The company responsible for keeping London's sewers moving is Thames Water, and they now employ a team of thirty-nine "flushers" to keep the city's sewers moving and blockage free.

All flushers are equipped with gas monitors and emergency breathing kits due to the constant threat of methane and hydrogen sulfide poisoning, but it is the fatbergs that are their real enemy.

Navigating their way through the maze of sewers beneath the feet of Londoners, the team of flushers are armed with shovels to dig out the fat blockages. They know the worst hot spots, and the sewers beneath Leicester Square are one of the worst. The area contains a large number of fast-food restaurants that illegally dump great quantities of used cooking oil. At one point, the team removed enough solidified fat to fill nine of London's iconic double-decker buses.

The flushers are now so expert in their field that they can identify old fat from the more yellowish new fat, but it's not all nastiness. The teams are very aware of the city's routine and say that at certain times of the day you can experience very different scents. For example, in the mornings when people are showering before work or school, they say that London's sewer network begins to smell of perfume. Likewise, Monday mornings seem to be the popular time for housework and the sewers start to smell strongly of bleach.

YOUNG SCIENTIST ACTIVITY
The Great Cooking Oil–Water Switch

This activity will show you how to completely switch a container of cooking oil with a container of water without spilling a drop.

EQUIPMENT NEEDED:

One outer case of a cereal box

One pair of scissors

Two beakers that are exactly the same size

Water

Cooking oil

One helper and some outside space

INSTRUCTIONS:

1. This experiment is best done outdoors as it can get messy, but practice will make you more expert. (An outdoor picnic table is perfect.)

2. Take the cereal box cardboard and the scissors and cut out a square with sides of approximately 4 inches long (10 cm). The square needs to be wide enough to cover the opening of the beakers you are using.

3. Take the beakers and fill one with cooking oil and the other with water. (Make sure both are filled equally.)

4. Put the cardboard on top of the beaker of water. Now for the tricky bit! Holding the cardboard firmly against the beaker of water, quickly flip it upside down with the cardboard now at the bottom and the bottom of the beaker pointing in the air.

5. Now place both the cardboard and the beaker of water on top of the beaker filled with oil. If the cardboard moves at this point, the game is over.

6. Now hold both beakers still; here's where your helper comes in. While you keep the beakers perfectly still, your helper must slowly and carefully pull the cardboard sideways and begin to create an opening between the two beakers. Watch what happens.

Science Factoid

As the cardboard is pulled across the beakers further and further, the oil begins to bubble upward into the water beaker and the water starts to run down into the oil beaker. As the water is heavier than the cooking oil, it flows downward under gravity's pull. The force of this downward flow forces the lighter oil upward. The perfect switcheroo!

Not Smoke, Not Fog, This is Smog

I like human beings, and I think everyone should at least get to know one if you can. They can be funny, charming and, in some cases, highly intelligent, but on the downside they can really make a mess of the place—littering after a picnic, spraying graffiti on walls or just having a bedroom is enough to cause havoc.

On a much bigger scale, groups of humans can make really big messes. In "urban areas" (the words boring geographers use to describe cities or built-up places, with lots of people) there are lots of people who like to do lots of things. As more people move to cities, they grow and become bigger. That means more factories, offices and vehicles, and that means more fumes and pollution.

As you've already discovered in this book, scientists enjoy making new words for everything. They do this so that at dinner parties they can sound more intelligent than anyone else and in doing so, make you want to scream for help. When scientists first discovered the smoky fog-like pollution that blanketed cities, they weren't happy to simply call it a smoke or a fog, instead they saw it as the perfect opening for a new science word. They then took:

SMOKE and FOG
remove the
OKE and the F
to leave SM + OG
making SMOG

Ever since that day, "smog" has been the word used to describe the dirty, smoky pollution that affects the world's big cities, which produce huge amounts of it.

WHEEZY DOES IT!

Smog is formed in exactly the same way as fog. Minute hygroscopic (science-speak for tiny particles that attract water) particles in the air such as soot, dust and smoke attract to water vapor, which creates the hazy low-lying cloud. It is produced by the burning of fossil fuels from cars, factories and airplanes.

PEA SOUP, SIR?

After a number of periods of heavy smog in London during the nineteenth and twentieth centuries, the occurrence of smog was christened "pea soup" because of its thick appearance and greenish color—YUCK!

TOP SMOG FACTS

- In December 1952, smog in London was said to be responsible for the death of over 4,000 people, although modern research has indicated that the figure was actually much higher.

- In Los Angeles there are almost 100 days per year when the air quality is classed as "very unhealthy."

- The people of Mexico City are believed to have some of the worst air quality in the world. One scientist remarked that breathing the air of Mexico City was the same as smoking up to 60 cigarettes a day! Worse still, scientific tests of the city's air have found significant amounts of fecal matter are breathed in everyday.

- Smog can even destroy and damage synthetic materials. It can cause leather to become brittle and rubber to lose its elasticity and begin cracking.

- Agriculture is also hurt by smog. Soybeans, wheat, tomatoes, peanuts, lettuce and cotton are all subject to pollution when exposed to smog.

TRIVIA COULD I HAVE TWO GAS MASKS AND A CLUB SANDWICH, PLEASE?

Smog is a major problem in most cities around the world. So much so that some clever urbanites (science-speak for people who live in cities) are cashing in on the horrible health risks. In Peking, China, cunning business people have spotted a market opportunity.

In 1995, three "oxygen bars" opened up in the city. The bars offered customers the chance to sit and enjoy a bite to eat, a cool drink and the rental of your very own oxygen mask to recover from the difficulties of trying to breathe the smoke-filled air all day!

Death by Methane Burps

Deep below the Arctic ice sheets are huge fields of a gas called "methane clathrate." The "clathrate" is used to describe methane locked within ice crystals. Methane is, of course, a very powerful greenhouse gas, and if large amounts of it were released into the atmosphere, it could well signal the end for the planet. Luckily for you though, this gassy nuisance is locked away nicely below the ice in polar regions and most stores are simply too deep to reach the surface.

PHEW! THAT'S OKAY THEN

Not really! You see what I didn't mention was that in the Siberian Arctic at the northernmost part of Russia, the methane deposits are very close to the surface. In fact, they are only stopped from releasing into the atmosphere by a layer of ice known as the "permafrost." Permafrost is the scientific term for "permanent frost covering." In other words, a frost that never melts.

PHEW! THAT'S OKAY THEN. WE'RE SAVED 'CAUSE THE FROST NEVER MELTS.

Ah, well! That's not exactly correct either. You see, scientists say that because humans are warming the planet by driving cars, overheating factories and letting cows fart too much, we are weakening the permafrost and it is starting to melt and thin. This situation could result in what is called "a methane gun"—where so much methane is released that there is a runaway global warming event that can't be stopped, just like a bullet from a gun—and that means "time's up" for most life on Earth.

HOW?

Some scientists believe that past methane "burps" escaping from the sea floor into the atmosphere caused rapid climate changes during and at the end of the last Ice Age. These methane "burps" raised the temperature of the planet by around 10° F (6° C)—a level of heating that would probably see all of us kiss the planet goodbye.

YOUNG SCIENTIST ACTIVITY
The Mysterious "Climbing" Water

It's not just methane and gases that can escape from deep underground. With this activity, you can witness water "climbing" from a seemingly tight spot before arriving at another. Let's take a look:

EQUIPMENT NEEDED:

One cereal bowl

Two sheets of absorbent kitchen towels

One glass

Water

INSTRUCTIONS:

1. To ensure there is no spillage, this activity is probably best carried out set inside the bathtub.

2. Place the cereal bowl and the glass very close to one another in the bottom of an empty bathtub.

3. Take the glass and fill it using the bath tap before placing it back beside the bowl.

4. Now take the paper towels and twist them in the same way you would wring out a wet towel. This creates a coiled piece of towel—a bit like a rope. Finally, bend the coiled kitchen towel in the middle and place one end into the glass of water with the other end reaching into the bowl.

Science Factoid

In just a few minutes, the towel will have water traveling along it. Over time, the water will start to appear in the bottom of the bowl. This will continue until the water is split about half and half between the two containers. The kitchen towel has many tiny air spaces and the water moves into these spaces in a process called "capillary action." Capillary action is the upward movement of water, and the best example in nature is the classic structure of a plant that takes water via its roots and moves that water upward through the rest of the plant. As a result, much of the water in the glass in your experiment is able to "climb" out and into the bowl.

OMG! It's an OMZ

You might be forgiven for thinking there is no oxygen in our oceans, but you'd be very wrong. Oxygen in our oceans has been an essential ingredient for marine life to evolve since the first oceans started to form over 3.8 billion years ago, but today there is growing evidence that oxygen levels in our oceans can fall so low that most animals would be unable to survive. The "choking" of the Earth's oceans is something that human beings are not only contributing to but need to watch out for.

The average amount of dissolved oxygen in our oceans is about 0.22 fluid ounces (6.5 ml) of oxygen for every liter of water, and this figure drops rapidly with greater depths in the ocean. As a result, seawater deeper than 160 feet (50 m) can actually be harmful to most fish life.

Worse still, when the concentration of dissolved oxygen falls from 30 percent of normal levels to just 1 percent, this is a seriously life-threatening condition known as "hypoxia."

The scientists of the world are becoming very concerned about oxygen-poor areas of the ocean they call "hypoxic dead zones," and since 2004, the number of documented dead zones has more than doubled.

Dead zones do occur naturally, but many are caused by chemicals from fertilizers used in farming washing off the land and into the sea. Farmers feel pressured into using the fertilizers to increase the number and size of the produce they farm. The problem is that these fertilizers boost the reproduction and growth of water-based algal blooms and these, in turn, greatly reduce the oxygen levels in our oceans and pose a threat to other marine life.

The naturally occurring Oxygen Minimum Zones or OMZs are normally found at ocean depths of 2,000–4,000 feet (600–1,200 m). These are zones in which oxygen levels are permanently lowered to less than 10 percent of surface levels. However, scientists believe we are witnessing an expansion of these enormous hypoxic zones.

Natural dead zones or OMZs can be found in the Gulf of Mexico, both U.S. seaboards, around the Japanese islands and in the Baltic and North Seas. The bigger concern is that due to man's farming practices and fertilizer use we are seeing these dead zones (in which fish cannot survive) growing by more than 1.5 million square miles (4 million km²).

Such growth has major implications for marine life on Earth and our continued food supply.

YOUNG SCIENTIST ACTIVITY
Hot versus Cold

The oceans of the world vary greatly. In particular, ocean temperatures can show major differences when affected by hot and cold ocean currents. With this activity, you will look at the science of hot and cold water, and see how temperature makes water act in different ways.

EQUIPMENT NEEDED:

Two drinking glasses

One eye dropper

Hot water

Cold water

One bottle of food coloring

INSTRUCTIONS:

1. Take both drinking glasses. Fill the first to the top with hot water. Then fill the second with exactly the same amount of cold water.

2. Now take your eye dropper and place it into the food coloring so that you have a few drops of colored liquid.

3. Place a single drop of the food coloring into both of the glasses very quickly. (Your quick speed is essential.) Watch what happens.

Science Factoid

Look at both glasses close up. You should notice that the food coloring spreads out much faster in the hot water than it does in the cold water. This is because the tiny molecules in the hot water are moving at a faster rate, which then spreads the food coloring in that glass at a faster speed. While those in the cold move at a slower speed, proving that hot and cold waters act differently.

Crazy Chemistry

We all love the idea of acting like a nutty professor and digging out our chemistry sets to blow things up or make things foam up or simply change color. Those are pretty harmless and really good fun, but what if chemistry got a whole lot bigger? Badder? Very messed-up? In this chapter you'll discover what happens when chemistry goes crazy. Oh! It's probably best if you pull on a full biohazard suit right here before you risk exposure to any life-threatening substances.

MAD HATTERS AND BACKWARD WALKING CATS

Way back in 1932 in the sleepy fishing town of Minamata Bay in Japan a large chemical factory opened to manufacture drugs and industrial products. The company produced mercury (a very dangerous and toxic

heavy metal) as a waste by-product, which it would simply dump directly into the bay to get rid of.

It continued to do this for more than 30 years alongside the local fishermen who lived on shellfish and clams they caught from the bay.

Then in 1953, the residents of Minamata started to notice some very strange things happening in their town. Firstly, the local cats and dogs that fed on the fish scraps from the docks of the bay began to act very weird. The cats were seen walking backward. They, like the dogs, would also suffer from strange convulsions, foaming at the mouth, and some even started flinging themselves into the ocean to die. Crows would crash wildly into the rocks and others simply dropped dead from the sky.

Worse was to come as the residents also began to suffer alarming symptoms. People complained of numbness in their limbs, loss of speech and hearing, and others began to shout out uncontrollably. These symptoms were all clear signs that the people and animals of Minamata Bay had suffered severe mercury poisoning from the local daily diet of contaminated seafood. The mercury in their diet had penetrated the nervous system.

The behavior of the people of Minamata Bay were clear signs to doctors of a very old disease once common in England called "mad-hatter disease." The name came from the outbreak of mercury poisonings in the 1800s that drove mad the specialists who worked with mercury to treat the felt and fur they used on hats. These specialists were called "hatters," and once the patterns of insanity were recognized to be linked to their trade, the phrase *"S/he's as mad as a hatter"* was coined.

That alongside knives and bombs, thermometers containing mercury are banned from all airplanes because the deadly chemical can also eat its way through the aluminium walls of the aircraft.

CAREFUL CHEMICALS!

- During the "Cold War" between the United States and Russia, both countries developed a weapon that had in it the same potato blight mold that devastated the Irish population during the Great Famine.

- In Brazil, they produce a product called "bromelain," which is used to soften or "tenderize" tough meat, but it is so strong that if the factory workers who produce it don't wear industrial gloves it would eat through the flesh of their hands.

- In South Africa, bank robbers should beware as many of their ATMs are fitted with pepper spray, which is shot out into the eyes of anyone thought to be tampering with or vandalizing the machine. While the perpetrator writhes in agony, the machine sends a call to the local police to come and pick up the robber.

YOUNG SCIENTIST ACTIVITY
How to Blow Up a Balloon Using Chemistry

Using clever chemistry in this experiment, you will inflate a balloon without ever needing to blow it up yourself.

EQUIPMENT NEEDED:

One small, see-through soda bottle

One spoonful of sugar

One small balloon

One packet of yeast

Warm water

INSTRUCTIONS:

1. Take the small soda bottle and fill it with around one inch (3 cm) of warm water.

2. Take your packet of yeast and empty it slowly into the bottle; stir the mixture.

3. Add a spoonful of sugar and stir once more.

4. Blow up the balloon several times and stretch it in your hands (this will make it easier to inflate). Fit the balloon over the top of the soda bottle.

5. Let the bottle sit in a warm place like a radiator for about 30 minutes. If the bottle is well sealed and if the yeast has the right conditions, the balloon will inflate all on its own.

Science Factoid

The yeast is made up of tiny microorganisms who are very hungry. When mixed with the warm water and sugar, the yeast starts to eat the sugar. As it does, it releases a gas called carbon dioxide. This gas fills the bottle first and then the balloon, as the yeast creates more and more of the stuff. If it generates enough gas, the balloon will fully inflate.

The Coral Quarrel

The Earth's coral reefs are home to around a quarter of all marine species and because of this great diversity of life, some scientists refer to them as "the rain forests of the ocean." Most coral reefs are built from stony corals—these underwater structures are made from calcium carbonate that the corals produce themselves to create a hard exterior that supports and protects their bodies. This unique combination of living creature and stony exterior has made coral reefs some of the largest living structures on the planet. The Great Barrier Reef, off the Australian coast, for example, is more than 1,243 miles (2,000 km) long.

CAN I HAVE SOME BRAIN CORAL, PLEASE?

Coral can grow in a vast range of different shapes. Some of these include sea fans, sea pens, sea whips, brain coral, pillars, organ pipes and staghorn coral to name just a few.

IN TROUBLE

Coral reefs are in big danger all around the planet due to human activities such as farming, pollution, over-fishing, climate change and even our use of sunscreen—yes, sunscreen.

Around 10 percent of the world's coral reefs are now dead and a further 60 percent of the world's reefs are endangered. This figure rises again to 80 percent if you look at the world's worst hit areas in Southeast Asia. It is estimated that if damaging human activities continue to "bleach" the coral, alongside the warming of oceans due to global warming, coral reefs will be nonexistent by 2050.

WHAT'S HAPPENING?

Scientists aren't fully aware of the long-term impacts of coral bleaching, but they do know for certain that bleaching leaves corals weakened to diseases. The process also stunts their growth, and affects their reproduction. The use of estrogen in many of our chemicals is "feminizing" much of the male coral, which leaves the coral unable to reproduce more new coral. Worse still could be the impact of your sunscreen on the coral. Recent studies have discovered the chemicals in some of our sunscreens are also attacking the coral. Scientists found that four ingredients in sun protection products can reawaken dormant viruses in the algae that live inside reef-building coral species.

These algae are called "zooxanthellae," and they are essential to coral survival as they provide the coral with food energy through the process of photosynthesis and help give the coral its healthy color. Without these little guys, the coral bleaches, turns white in color and dies.

TRIVIA The scientific studies estimate that between 4,000 to 6,000 metric tons of sunscreen wash off the bodies of swimmers every year in our oceans, and kills up to 10 percent of coral across the planet. It's not all bad news though . . . there are many eco-friendly creams on the market which won't hurt the coral . . . just check carefully to make sure you've got the right one!

YOUNG SCIENTIST ACTIVITY
Good G-Reef!

You already know that coral reefs are protected by a hard stony material made of calcium carbonate. Sea shells are made up from the same stuff, and with this experiment you will be able to re-create some of the threats our coral reefs face.

EQUIPMENT NEEDED:

One metal spoon

One old newspaper

Two jam jars

One glass of vinegar

One glass of water

A small collection of sea shells

INSTRUCTIONS:

1. Take the two empty jam jars. Fill one with the glass of vinegar and fill the other with the glass of water.

2. Place some shells in each jar and leave undisturbed for 7 days.

3. After the 7 days, remove the shells from the jars and place them on the newspaper to dry out, putting the shells in piles according to which jar they were in.

4. Now take the metal spoon and hit each separate pile of shells as hard as you can.

Science Factoid

The two piles of shells now act differently. The shells that were placed in the jar of water for 7 days remain as they normally would, but the shells placed in the vinegar should start to crack and break up fairly easily. These shells have been affected by the vinegar, which is an acid. The acid starts to dissolve the calcium carbonate in the shells, which weakens its structure and allows it to break up more easily.

ASK YOUR DOCTOR IF DRACULIN IS RIGHT FOR YOU

Messed Up Chemical Names

A University in England in 1997 decided to put all their scientific brainpower together to create a list of the most weirdly named chemicals they could find. These silly scientists did quite well in undertaking their odd experiment. The list below contains just a few crazy chemicals:

Penguinone

CHEMICAL	WHAT IT IS
Crapinon	This sounds very unpleasant and is a drug that can cause constipation.
Vomitoxin	Again, horrible-sounding and is, in fact, a toxin used to put animals off their food.
Penguinone	A little cuter chemical compound which, in certain views, looks like ... well ... a penguin!
D.A.M.N.	The chemical name given to a compound which is linked to the Cyanide family.
Miraculin	Taken from the miracle fruit, this little wonder can make the food you eat turn from sour to sweet.
Draculin	A blood-thinning chemical taken from vampire bats and named after Dracula.
Traumatic Acid	Although it sounds terrible, this compound actually helps heal damaged plants.
D.E.A.D.	This little beauty is dangerous in so many ways. It is highly likely any contact with it could result in you ending up ... erm ... dead.

YOUNG SCIENTIST ACTIVITY
Scary Bloodbath

Although some chemicals can have pretty dumb names, some can do some very cool stuff. This activity will show you how to make your very own blood, and scare the pants off your friends.

EQUIPMENT NEEDED:

One bar of soap

Two laxative pills such as Ex-Lax

One metal spoon

One tablespoon rubbing alcohol

One bowl

INSTRUCTIONS:

1. Place the two pills into the empty bowl.

2. Use the spoon to crush the pills.

3. Pour the rubbing alcohol into the bowl.

4. Rub the mixture over both hands and wait for your hands to dry.

5. Once your hands are completely dry, wash the mixture off with the soap and find a friend who you can totally freak out.

Science Factoid

Your scary bloodbath is caused by a clever chemical reaction. The laxative pills have a chemical inside called "phenolphthalein." When mixed with a base or alkali it turns bright red in color. The soap contains a strong alkali that is released when water is added to it, which turns your hands blood red.

The Worst Scientist in the World Ever

With over 7 billion people now on the planet, it might be understandable if we started to influence the natural workings of the Earth, but one man almost single-handedly destroyed us all with crazy experiment after crazy experiment.

Thomas Midgley Junior was born in 1889, the son of Thomas Midgley Senior, an inventor. Little junior followed in his father's footsteps and grew up to become a mechanical engineer and chemist.

In 1916, Midgley began working at General Motors, and by the end of 1921, he discovered a mixture of chemicals called "tetraethyl lead" or TEL for short that, when added to ordinary gasoline, prevented the juddering or knocking in car engines. Midgley went on to win several notable awards for his noise-reducing invention, but failed to mention the fact that the lead added to the gasoline was capable of irreparable damage to the brain and nervous system, which results in blindness, convulsions, madness and even death—almost 20 of the workers in General Motors factories died from lead poisoning.

KILLING THE ATMOSPHERE

Not satisfied with lead poisoning, Midgley turned his attentions to the great 1920s problem of refrigerators. Back then they used very dangerous gases, and Midgley wanted a breathable, non-flammable gas that could keep food cold. He came up with what we know today as CFCs or scientifically referred to as "chlorofluorocarbons." Unfortunately, it took more than half a century for scientists to realize that good old CFCs had literally eaten through our atmosphere and created a giant hole in the ozone layer.

Ozone is a type of oxygen that, at ground level, is classed as a pollutant but is actually helpful in the upper atmosphere because it absorbs dangerous ultraviolet rays, which can help reduce cancer-causing sunlight that affects humans and other species. Midgley's invention created a hole in the ozone layer that was 6.5 million square miles (17 million km^2) in size—an area larger than the whole of Antarctica.

If Midgley's inventions so far weren't bad enough, in 1951 he became severely ill and debilitated. To help him move around, he invented a pulley system to help him in and out of bed. Alas, several years later the very same pulley invention backfired and brought an end to one of the worst inventors in the world ever!

YOUNG SCIENTIST ACTIVITY
Destroying the Ozone Layer

This activity will let you create a miniature planet Earth with its own ozone layer under attack from CFCs. The bottle is the planet itself, the gum acts as the ozone layer and the hot water does the work of the CFCs.

EQUIPMENT NEEDED:

One kettle of hot water

One stick of gum

One small soda bottle

INSTRUCTIONS:

1. Take the stick of gum and chew it until it is soft and stretchy.

2. Remove the gum from your mouth, and roll it into a small, flat circle that is big enough to cover the top of the soda bottle.

3. Take the soda bottle and fill it using the very hot (but not boiling) water from the kettle.

4. Take the gum "cap" and seal the top of the bottle. Make sure there are no holes in the gum "cap."

5. Finally, make sure the bottle is full enough so that the water and gum are in contact with each other, and watch what happens.

Science Factoid

As the water and the gum "cap" come into contact, the gum starts to lose its elastic qualities and holes start to form just as holes form in the real ozone layer. As the experiment continues, the gum "cap" breaks apart completely.

Gum

Agricultural Fiascoes

A Real Math Problem:
Humans + Cows + Farts = Global Warming

Most of the 7 billion of us on Earth are meat eaters. We have been since cavemen times when we roamed around with clubs and literally whacked our food over the head before dragging it home for the family to feast on. Back then "fast food" simply meant you had to run a little faster to catch dinner.

Nowadays things are a lot different. Most of us would not have the first idea how to stalk a deer or hunt a rabbit. In fact, most of us are now totally dependent on stores and food outlets to provide us with the food we eat, and that's beginning to cause us problems . . . big, loud smelly problems!

The meat we eat, especially beef, is contributing to global warming. Yes, the much-loved super-sized, super-duper McWhopper sandwich is affecting the planet. Let's take a closer look.

INSANE ME-THANE

Methane is a naturally occurring gas on Earth. It is released when plants, vegetables and animals begin to decay. The problem is that it is also released from certain animals' waste matter and wind. The guilty animals are those who feed on grasses such as sheep, goats, bison and public enemy number one— cows. This grassy diet has a very gassy outcome, and that's why cow farts and burps are deadlier than the human kind.

Methane belongs to the greenhouse gases family, which trap heat in the atmosphere, gradually making the planet hotter. Methane is particularly dangerous in that it is about 25 times better at trapping heat than carbon dioxide (another greenhouse gas). This fact plus the growing number of humans on Earth plus our growing desire to eat more and more red meat means we are breeding more cows and that means more poop, more farts and more burps = more methane!

HOLY COW!

You might just be thinking, how can a few farm animals make a big difference to our planet? But let's do the math:

A single cow can release over 220 pounds (100 kg) of methane per year (that's the same weight as a large man), multiplied by the number of farting cows, sheep, goats, etc., which is more than 1 billion, = more than 80 million tons of methane released into the atmosphere each year . . . that's a lot of gas floating around up there!

THE GOOD NEWS

We can't just de-cow the planet. It wouldn't be fair to the cows, and we still need them to survive, but we can take some important steps:

1. Fart-reduction programs. Scientists in Ireland and the United Kingdom believe they have come up with a way to reduce methane emissions from cows and other animals by 50 percent. Gas from animal farts and burps accounts for one-fifth of the world's methane emissions—that's a lot of gas. However, scientists found that feeding animals on a low-fiber diet actually halved the amount of methane released.

2. Mix up your diet a bit. Medical science shows that reducing the red meat in your diet actually makes you fitter and healthier. It also reduces cow demand, which directly reduces cow poop and farts = a healthier planet all round.

3. Move the poop indoors. This is a process called "harvesting" and means the poop that normally lies outdoors and releases methane into the atmosphere is collected and can be used to generate renewable electricity. This acts as an alternative to fossils fuels, which also contribute to the greenhouse gases.

4. Future options—the test-tube burger. Scientists believe they are not too far away from using special stem cells from a cow, multiplying them a billion times or so to create a "muscle" of beef, and creating their very own lab-grown burger. Freaky as it may sound, a study carried out by Oxford University found that this process would use:

- Between 35 and 60 percent less energy than current burger production techniques.

- 98 percent less land.

YOUNG SCIENTIST ACTIVITY
A Gassy Explosion

Gassy emissions are released from a huge number of things on Earth. With this activity, you'll have a simple, messy and gassy explosion.

EQUIPMENT NEEDED:

One outdoor space (This will be quite messy. So, outdoors is best for this one.)

A set of old clothes or overalls

One large bottle of clear soda

One bottle of food coloring (bright colors have the best effect)

Some sheets of kitchen towel

INSTRUCTIONS:

1. Put on a set of old clothes or overalls.

2. In your outdoor space, create a blanket of kitchen towels to soak up most of the explosion.

3. Now, unscrew the cap of the soda bottle and add the food coloring until the entire bottle is a bright color.

4. Screw the cap back on as tightly as you can and shake the bottle up and down as hard as you can for about five seconds.

5. Unscrew the cap a little, holding the bottle away from you, and watch it go!

Science Factoid

Fizzy soda is jam-packed with a gas called carbon dioxide, which remains invisible while the cap is sealed. Bubbles don't form because the pressure inside the bottle keeps the carbon dioxide dissolved and hidden in the soda. Once the bottle is shaken and the cap opened, the bubbles rush upward as the pressure in the bottle drops. Under falling pressure, the bubbles grow and expand in an explosive fountain. The color simply makes it easier for us to see the sticky science.

Weird Animal Groupings

By now you should be realizing that some scientists aren't that smart and that they can do some pretty dumb things. Unfortunately, the animal kingdom has not managed to escape the clutches of these scientists, and when it comes to naming groups of animals you will be entertained to say the least. Most of us wouldn't bat an eyelid about calling a group of sheep "a flock" or a group of elephants "a herd," but what about an animal grouping known as "a murder," "a pandemonium" or "a carload"? Read on to hear about some truly weird animal groupings.

GROUP NAME	ANIMAL
A Posse	of Turkeys
A Mutation	of Thrushes
A Cloud	of Bats
A Business	of Flies
A Bike	of Hornets
A Carload	of Monkeys
A Lounge	of Lizards
A Murder	of Magpies
A Pandemonium	of Parrots
A Bouquet	of Pheasants
A Storytelling	of Ravens
A Crash	of Rhinoceroses
A Congress	of Salamanders
A Wreck	of Seabirds
A Fever	of Stingrays

TRIVIA The names scientists have given to animal groupings may seem downright weird, but some of the scientific studies conducted on animals are right up there in the strangeness stakes. Amazingly, studies into which is the best floor of a high-rise building to throw a living cat from are actually very common. Records show that some cats have fallen more than thirty stories without injury, and in 1987, the American Veterinary Medical Association produced a paper that studied more than 130 cat falls from high-rise buildings in New York City. The average fall was just over five stories, with a survival rate of around 90 percent. There was also clear evidence that the further a cat fell, the higher its survival rate . . . but why?

Cats have what scientists call "a non-fatal terminal velocity" that is around 60 mph (100 kmph). At this speed, cats stop accelerating through the air as their body weight and the air resistance around them balance out. This results in the cat's body acting more like a parachute than a rapidly accelerating object hurtling toward the ground.

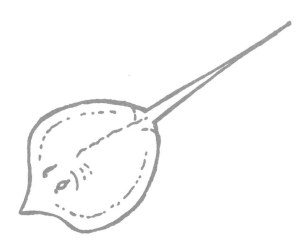

A Poop and a Pee Makes a Nice Coffee

Yes, believe it or not humans have some strange uses for waste products. I know it sounds really messed-up, but across the planet, people use pee and poop in a whole range of mind-boggling ways that you would never have imagined.

WOW! YOU SMELL LIKE C*@P

The expensive and beautiful scent of your mom's perfume may make her feel wonderful. However, if she knew the messed-up science behind her favorite fragrance, she might have second thoughts about ever buying it again. The ingredient ambergris is regularly used in perfumes because of its sweet, earthy aroma but its origins are a lot less attractive. Ambergris occurs naturally as a secretion in the intestines of the sperm whale. It is also sometimes found in their stomachs.

UGLY EXIT ROUTES

Ambergris makes its way into the world in two ways:

1. It's pooped out of the whale as fecal matter.

2. Ambergris that is too large to get through the intestines of the whale is coughed up through the mouth; in other words, it is whale barf.

THERE'S GOLD IN THEM THERE POOPS!

Whale poop can be found floating upon the sea or in the sand near the coast. It appears as solid, waxy lump and a lucky beachcomber who finds just 1 pound (0.45 kg) of the stuff could earn as much as $10,000 for it. Experts often refer to ambergris as the "gold of the sea," and if you compare the like for like values of the whale poop and gold, it's not hard to see why. Ambergris sells at roughly $20 a gram while gold currently sells for $30 a gram. Recently, in southern Australia a lucky couple bagged themselves over $300,000 after stumbling on a 32-pound (14.5 kg) chunk of whale poop.

POOP AND PEE DISHES

Here is just a "flavor" of the uses of poop and pee delicacies from around the world:

- A restaurant in Hailin city in northeast China was raided and closed by authorities in 2005 for listing stir-fried tiger meat on its menu. The Siberian tiger is one of the 10 most endangered animals in the world. Police later found out that the "tiger meat" was actually donkey meat soaked with tiger urine to give it a "special" flavor . . . mmm . . . tasty.

- Coke? Pepsi? Cow Pee? India's leading Hindu cultural group, has developed "Gau Jal" or "Cow Water," at its research center on the river Ganges, and hopes the drink made of cow urine will be marketed as a "healthy" alternative to Coke and Pepsi.

- The extremely rare and very expensive, Kopi Luwak coffee from the Philippines is produced in a very unique way. Wild cat-like creatures called civets feed on the red coffee cherries that contain the beans. The civets digest the flesh of the coffee cherries but pass the beans inside, leaving their stomach enzymes to go to work on the beans. They are then pooped out, collected and washed. This process apparently adds to the coffee's prized aroma and flavor. It is estimated that only around 1,000 pounds (450 kg) of civet coffee makes it to market each year, and 1 pound (0.45 kg) of the stuff can cost you up to $600 in some parts of the world. Some fans are willing to pay up to $100 a cup. Coffee anyone?

TRIVIA **EXPLODING POOP!**

In 2007, in the U.S., farmers were scratching their heads about a strange problem occurring on their farms . . . exploding poop! The pig farmers had discovered a worrying pattern that the waste stored in their manure pits was exploding, with dangerous results. One event in Iowa resulted in the deaths of more than 1,500 pigs and hospitalized the farmer. Other blasts raised roofs and blew out the windows of buildings that contained the pits. Chuck Clanton, a professor at the University of Minnesota began an investigation into the strange occurrences and discovered that just before an explosion, pits would bubble up into a violent foam. He later found out that the foam held and then released large amounts of the highly flammable gas methane. Clanton knew that the methane was produced by bacteria in the pits, but couldn't work out what was causing the foam. Then he turned to the livestock feed given to the pigs called DDGS (Distillers Dried Grains with Solubles). He discovered that some of the DDGS contained fatty acids that are used to make soap and, of course, the soap made the bubbles. As a result, the large amounts of foam being created trapped the naturally occurring methane until it reached dangerous levels and BOOM!!! . . . a poop time bomb!

YOUNG SCIENTIST ACTIVITY
Multi-Colored Milk

Milk can be just perfect in coffee, but milk and soap are a lot more fun. You can make a whole rainbow of colors with this simple activity.

EQUIPMENT NEEDED:

One large plate

1/4 cup milk (whole or 2% fat milk works best)

A mixture of food colorings, e.g. blue, green
(the more colors, the better)

Dish-washing soap

Cotton swabs

INSTRUCTIONS:

1. Take the large plate and pour just enough milk on to the plate to completely cover the bottom to a depth of around a quarter of an inch (less than 1 cm).

2. Now add a single drop of each of your colors of food coloring to the milk. Try to ensure that the drops are close together near the middle of the plate.

3. Take a cotton swab and simply touch the milk with the swab. Do not stir the milk.

4. Then take a drop of liquid dish-washing soap on the other end of the cotton swab. Place the soap-covered end of the cotton swab back in the middle of the milk and hold it there for approximately 15 seconds and watch what happens.

5. Continue to add soap to the tip of the cotton swab and repeat. You will see that the colors in the milk continue to move even when the swab is taken away from the milk.

Science Factoid

The secret to the science in this experiment is held inside the drop of soap. It weakens the chemical bonds that hold the proteins and fats in the milk together. The soap molecules attach to the fats in the milk and cause them to move, bend and twist in all directions as the soap molecules rush to bond with the fat molecules. As all this crazy science carries on, the food coloring molecules are knocked and bumped around in all directions providing an easy way to observe all of the otherwise invisible chemistry.

Ligers, Tigons and Bears ... Oh My!

"**H**ybrids" are the scientific name for plants and animals that cross or mix with a species that has a close genetic link with it. In truth, in the natural world, hybrids are very rare. That's until humans wade in—we're not happy to have boring old lions, tigers and bears. No! We need mix it up a little around here ... make it a little more interesting and, oh, boy have we done that. Let's take a look at some of science's major mix-ups.

LIGERS AND TIGONS

Lions and tigers have a very close genetic makeup, which has resulted in scientists mixing them up a little. But what's the difference between the two?

To make a liger you need this simple equation:

Take one male lion + one female tiger = one new **Liger**

On the other hand, a tigon is pretty much a reverse of the process and the equation goes like this:

Take one male tiger + one female lion = one new **Tigon**

MIXED-UP BEARS: MEET THE GROLAR AND THE PIZZLY

A grolar bear and a pizzly bear are the products of a grizzly bear and a polar bear crossover and they differ just like ligers and tigons depending on the male/female mix.

SYNTHETIC BIOLOGY—A WHOLE NEW LEVEL OF MIXING

Back when *The Simpsons* movie hit the screen, it was quite funny for Homer to lift his new pet pig and walk it up the walls of his house singing "Spiderpig, Spiderpig" to the classic tune from the *Spider-Man* cartoons, but the whole idea of a half-pig, half-spider combination just seemed ridiculous. Well, the producers of the movie weren't that far away from a mix of creatures that is nothing short of incredible—the Spidergoat.

On a farm owned by Utah State University in the U.S. lives an incredible creature that is part goat, part spider. The little white female goat looks just like any other goat in the world, but Freckles is unlike any other creature ever seen in the history of Earth. She is the creation of Professor Lewis, a professor of genetics who calls the process for making Freckles "synthetic biology." He describes it as breeding animals to produce things that we humans want or need.

WHAT CAN IT DO FOR US?

The scientists want to produce miles and miles of dragline silk (the silk that spiders catch themselves with when they are falling). The silk is one of the strongest fibers known to man but it is not possible to "farm" spiders because they are very cannibalistic and will begin to eat one another. So, Professor Lewis and his team decided to remove the gene that controls the dragline silk from an orb-weaver spider and placed it into the DNA that controls milk production in the udders of the goats. As a result, when Freckles is milked, her milk is full of the spider-silk protein.

TWO QUARTS OF SILK MILK, PLEASE

That's just the beginning of the process. First, the team of scientists milk the spidergoats. They then heat the milk in the lab to leave behind only the silk proteins. They then lift out a single fiber of what is spider silk and spool it onto a reel. The long-term aim is to use this silk in medical operations such as ligament repair and other procedures. The team has already witnessed it used in medical procedures with great success.

OTHER MAD MIXTURES

Here are few other zany creatures that scientists have messed with:

Camel + Llama = **Cama**

Zebra + Donkey = **Zonkey**

Bison + Cow = **Beefalo**

False Killer Whale + Bottlenose Dolphin = **Wholphin**

Pollinating by Numbers

You can be forgiven for thinking that bees are just annoying striped little insects that do nothing other than bother you with their buzzing and savage you with their stings, but bees are incredibly important for mankind, and they are in very big trouble. Bee numbers are in huge decline all over the planet due to a phenomenon known as CCD or Colony Collapse Disorder. This basically means that bee colonies lose large numbers of their population, and as a result begin to collapse completely and die out.

Scientists believe that CCD is due to the wide use of pesticides by farmers and a recently discovered infection that spreads rapidly through bee colonies. It is estimated that over 30 percent of bees in North America have already been killed off.

BEE CAREFUL WITH YOUR CELL PHONE!

Yes! Believe it or not, recent scientific studies across the world have shown that cell phones and cell phone masts are contributing to a fall in bee numbers also. It is thought that the signals beamed out from the mast to the phones confuse the honeybees so much that it messes with their sense of direction, resulting in many bees getting totally lost when they leave their hive for a day's hard work. Since bees don't carry cell phones themselves, they can't phone mom to help them find their way home.

IT CAN'T BEE THAT BIG A DEAL?

Think about this—almost all the food crops that human beings live on come from crops that insects have pollinated. More importantly, bees are far and away the most efficient insect at doing this job. Without bees, most of the pollinating of plants and crops stops, and that means huge gaps in your food supply chain and starvation for billions of people. In fact, the problem has already gotten so bad in parts of the world that farmers in parts of China and Southeast Asia are now pollinating their plants and crops by hand. They do this using paint brushes with pollen on the end and some scientists jokingly describe this practice as "pollinating by numbers" just like good old painting by numbers!

On a serious note though, if bee numbers continue to fall, more and more farmers are going to have to reach for their paint brushes to ensure that we all get fed or else.

THE "ZOMBEE" APOCALYPSE

You may have heard of the zombie apocalypse but this is an invasion of an all new kind. "Zombees" are bees that have been infected by a parasitic fly. The infection is wiping out many bee colonies in North

America and causes the bees to fly around at nighttime before flying around aimlessly and then dying.

The scientists studying the virus and the zombees compare the parasitic fly's behavior to that seen in the sci-fi movie *Alien*. A small female fly first lands on the back of a honeybee and injects its eggs into the bee's abdomen, which later hatches into a batch of maggots. The maggots then eat out the inside of the bees. If you'd like to find out more about the spread of the zombee apocalypse or to become a zombee hunter go to www.zombeewatch.org.

YOUNG SCIENTIST ACTIVITY
Bee Nice

With this activity, you could make a big difference to the planet, help out our friends the bees and add some nice plants to your home. Even those of you that live in the city or an apartment can do something.

EQUIPMENT NEEDED:

One garden or outside space (even a small window ledge will do)

A good range of plants and flowers* (see the next page for the best varieties)

One garden trowel • One watering can • Water

INSTRUCTIONS:

1. Take whatever outside space you have and add some bee-friendly trees and plants. If you only have limited space, a small window-box garden is just as good.

2. Using the space you have, take your trowel and dig a hole in the soil large enough to house the base of your plant.

3. Add your plant to the hole and give it plenty of water before covering firmly with soil.

4. Repeat the process with your other trees and plants wherever you can.

5. Leave for nature and the bees to take their course.

Science Factoid

To help increase the honeybee populations, a garden planted with a wide variety of flowers is best to attract bees. Colorful plants are also good because these will attract more honeybees and also makes your garden look pretty.

FROM A TO BEE

Bees will prefer the most appealing plants in a close area. Scientists believe bees "plan" their journeys so that they are as efficient as they can be. So, if you pack as many bee-friendly species together in a close area you will reduce bee travel time between each flower and plant—giving more pollen and nectar and making for happy, buzzing bees.

*BEE FAVORITES

Trees

Some flowering trees have very high nectar content that bees like. The Korean Evodia is so bee-friendly some call it the "bee bee." Other bee favorites include crabapple and magnolia trees.

Plants

Bee balm flowers are colorful and are a good source of nectar. Other useful plants include buttercups, roses, geraniums and clematis. All of these have high nectar and pollen content.

Weeds

Humans don't like weeds but bees still find them useful. You might want to leave any white clover or dandelions alone as the bees really like these.

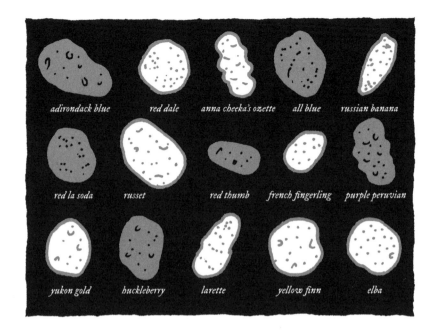

adirondack blue · red dale · anna cheeka's ozette · all blue · russian banana

red la soda · russet · red thumb · french fingerling · purple peruvian

yukon gold · huckleberry · larette · yellow finn · elba

Blasting our Biodiversity

Biodiversity is the scientific word for the wide and varied plant and animal species that populate our planet. Luckily, this planet has always been rich with endless types of different plants and animals, but humans have greatly threatened the future of the planet by wiping out many species. Worse still, some of those species could contain the miracle cure for some of our worst diseases. After all, we should really thank Mother Nature for some of our best medicines. Take a look at just a few miracle cures nature has given us.

THE FOOD ARK

The scientists and farmers of this planet are worried about our future. They estimate that to feed our rapidly growing population, we need to double our food production or else, but there's a major problem—the rate at which we grow food is not increasing quickly enough to keep pace with the exploding human population. Add into this equation the twin threats from climate change and ever-evolving new diseases that already threaten our food supplies and you've got a major global problem.

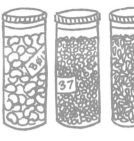

One hope for us all is Heritage Farm in Iowa, in the U.S. Here they are preparing for the future in a clever and unique way. The farmers of Heritage Farm are collecting and storing seeds rather than growing them, and they have grown into one of the largest "seed banks" in the country where seeds are cataloged and squirreled away. This project is dedicated to ensuring our future food supply because most of us have lost touch with where our food comes from and what exactly we are eating. We simply visit our local supermarket and pick what we want, but the supermarkets and others have hidden a secret from us about the future of food . . . it's heading for big trouble!

SPECIES LOSS

Most of us have heard about the loss of plants and animals in our rain forests, but have you heard anything about similar species loss from the list of foods you eat? I very much doubt it.

The truth is that food varieties all over the planet are facing extinction at a very rapid rate. Scientists believe that the U.S. has lost around 90 percent of its varieties of fruit and vegetable species. Likewise, in China the scale of loss has been similar for wheat varieties with only 10 percent remaining, and the same is happening everywhere.

WHAT'S THE BIG DEAL?

Well, we have basically made our range of food supplies narrower and narrower because we have farmed a small variety of foods. This concentration on just a small choice leaves our food supply very vulnerable to pests, diseases and climate change. If diseases were to take hold of the narrow range of food we rely on, we would have nothing else to rely on and that would spell global disaster.

Our best hope seems to lie with our friends at Heritage Farm and other similar schemes that have been described as "food arks." This name is intended to be similar to the ark Noah built in biblical times to save all of creatures on Earth. The story goes that Noah built the ark ahead of a great flooding that would have wiped out all life, but thankfully Noah's ark housed two of every creature and saved them from extinction. Heritage Farm specialists see their work in a similar way. They are preparing for the worst and stockpiling local, traditional seeds just in case they are needed to save the human race from mass extinction.

POTATO FAMINE—A WARNING

In Peru, South America, the humble potato was first farmed, and farmers there still grow thousands of different potato varieties. This not only creates different flavors and dishes, but creates a safety net if one or two varieties are lost. Over time, the Spanish brought the potato to Europe before it ended up in Ireland and the Irish became totally dependent on it. However, unlike the Peruvians, the Irish farmed only one variety—the lumper potato.

In 1845 spores of the deadly potato fungus spread across Ireland destroying all the lumpers and causing a famine that displaced and starved millions of people.

The same threats remain today, and the key to success for mankind will be to increase food production for our growing numbers while keeping as much variety in our food sources as possible. With just over 1,400 food arks dotted across the planet scientists are hopeful that we can weather any storm.

Trees—Please Don't Leaf!

Y ou can be forgiven for thinking trees are a bit boring. After all, unless you've got a tree house or a swing attached to one, they don't appear to do very much. Well, that's where you're wrong, because without trees this planet would be a completely lifeless ball of rock just spinning in space. Over one third of Earth's land surface is covered by forests that are vital for sustaining all life. These forests are filled to the brim with plants and animals that are essential for keeping humans alive but, of course, we are cutting them down at a rapid pace.

WHAT CAN A TREE DO FOR ME AND YOU?

Trees and other plants are often known as "Earth's lungs" because they absorb or breathe in billions of tons of carbon dioxide (which is harmful to us) and release or breathe out oxygen into the atmosphere (which living things need to breathe).

HOW DO THEY DO IT?

Plants are very clever because they can combine the carbon, from carbon dioxide in the air, with water and sunlight and turn it into sugars to feed them. This process makes oxygen, which is then released into the atmosphere. Scientists call this process "photosynthesis." Photosynthesis doesn't just clean the air, it also provides plants with the sugars they need for the energy to grow, and this is the second reason why trees and plants are essential.

OUR GLOBAL FOOD SUPPLY

Almost every animal and human on the planet rely on trees and plants for their food. As you read earlier, plants do a very clever chemistry trick using the sun's energy to make their own food. Plants are unique in their ability to do this, and, as a result, if we didn't have them we would all starve. Let's see how it works:

FOOD EXPERIMENT

INSTRUCTIONS

1. Take a bright, clear sunny day and find a large field.

2. Place in the large field: one human, one cow and one plant.

3. Remove from the field when the sun goes down.

4. Examine results—The human will probably be very red and blotchy from the sun, as well as dehydrated and very hungry. The cow will also probably need water, but if the field had grass, it will be okay. The plant will be perfectly healthy; it will have grown and made its own food.

The point is, no matter how long a cow or a human sits in the sun, they will never be able to carry out the clever chemistry trick those plants and trees do. They will just get red and dehydrated. So, plants and trees not only make our air safe to breathe, they are the starting point for our food chains. It works like this:

GRASS EATEN BY MOO COW EATEN BY HUMAN

Scientists call the animals that live on plants "herbivores" (remember the start of that word to help you, "herb" means "plant"). These animals are then eaten by "carnivores"—the scientific word for meat-eating animals. Without boring old trees and plants, there would be no herbivores for carnivores to eat and that would mean bye-bye human race.

HUMAN IMPACT

Scientists are worried that deforestation in our largest forests—the rain forests—could spell disaster for us in the future. One of our largest forests is the Amazon rain forest in South America. It is so big that it runs across nine countries and is around 2.3 million square miles (6 million km²). (That's enough forest to cover more than half of the entire continent of Europe). Experts believe the forest is so big and thick there may be people living in the forest who have never been in contact with the outside world. Worryingly, in the past 50 years, more than a fifth of the rain forest has been cut down or burned. Big companies cut the trees to sell the wood for building homes or making furniture, or to clear the land to grow crops and graze cattle.

Scientists believe that at this rate we are losing up to 100 species of plants and animals each day. Many of these species have never been discovered before and they may contain cures for our worst diseases and help make useful medicines.

ADDING TO CLIMATE CHANGE

Remember, at the start of this chapter you learned how forests recycle our air by soaking up carbon dioxide and breathing out fresh air. Of course, humans can be pretty dumb about the planet and had the bright idea of cutting all the trees down. This also speeds up climate change, as the Earth's forests absorb billions of tons of carbon dioxide gas each year, including about one-third that humans contribute with their cars, power stations and airplanes. And it's a Catch-22 situation because fewer trees = less carbon dioxide absorbed = more carbon dioxide in the atmosphere = more global warming, and so on.

YOUNG SCIENTIST ACTIVITY
How to Make Oxygen

With this activity, you will make the same oxygen the forests make each day but on a mini scale.

EQUIPMENT NEEDED:

One large see-through jar

Water

One leaf

Sunshine

A magnifying glass

INSTRUCTIONS:

1. Wait for a sunny day.

2. Take your large jar to the tap and fill it to the top with water.

3. Take your leaf and place it into the jar full of water.

4. Now take the jar and place it outdoors or directly on a window ledge where the sun can beam right inside the jar to the leaf.

5. Leave the jar in the sunshine for several hours before taking a closer look with your magnifying glass.

Science Factoid

After several hours in the sunshine, the leaf and the jar should be covered in tiny bubbles of air. This is evidence that leaves really are oxygen-making machines. The leaf is using the sunlight and carbon dioxide in the air to make its own food. The carbon dioxide enters the underside of the leaf and used is along with the sunlight to make a sugary energy for the plant. By the wonder of design, oxygen is released from the leaf as a by-product of this food-making process.

Let's Blow Up the North Pole

This was a very serious idea that some top weather scientists had back in the 1960s, and it was a plan that could have an impact far beyond the backyard of dear old Santa Claus. Most humans think the North and South Poles are just very large and very cold areas where not much happens except for a few penguins or polar bears hanging out on the ice, but the top and bottom of our planet are very important, and they work extremely hard at keeping the rest of the world at a comfortable temperature range.

WHITE, ALL RIGHT

The icy poles aren't bright white in color by a coincidence—they were designed that way to maximize their "albedo." This is science-speak (pronounced "al-bee-doh") and it is used to describe how reflective the surfaces on Earth are.

Earth's oceans and dark soils aren't very good at reflecting the sun's rays, so they have a very low albedo, which is around 10 percent. This means they absorb more heat from the sun than they reflect—a bit like wearing dark clothes on a hot day. Fresh snow has a very high albedo— around 85 percent or even more. That means icy areas like the North and South Poles act like giant mirrors, reflecting most of the sunlight they receive back into space. This process helps the entire planet stay cool—in just the same way that wearing white clothes keeps you cool on a summer's day. If all of the ice at the Earth's poles was to melt, the planet would be a much hotter place.

BOMB THE ARCTIC

Knowing how the poles worked to keep the Earth cool, in 1946 a British zoologist, Julian Huxley, told people that he would like to use nuclear bombs to blow up the Arctic ice cap to create a warmer climate and make areas that were not suitable for farming more farm-able. Huxley's plan never really took off until 1962, when the chief of science at the U.S. Weather Bureau, Harry Wexler, brought it up again. He wanted to use hydrogen bombs (10 to be exact) to obliterate the whole of the North Pole. Wexler's idea began to spread, and even the Russians believed the idea had legs and had many great benefits, including bringing rain to the dry and dusty Sahara where farming could spring up and an increase in trade through the previously frozen areas of the Arctic. The Russian scientists batted away concerns about the rise in global sea levels that melting the Greenland icecap would bring, saying sea levels would only rise a millimeter or two per year. Indeed, they went even further than Wexler and thought up a plan to create what they called "a Polar Gulf Stream," which would redirect warm water into the Arctic and cold water out of it via an enormous dam—a bit like giant hot and cold water taps. They said that this plan would balance temperatures between the Arctic and the equator so that all areas in between were roughly the same temperature, making previously harsh areas good for living, working and farming. Luckily, none of these crazy ideas came to pass and we, polar bears and Santa Claus can breathe easy for a little while longer. At least until another mad scientist comes along.

TRIVIA For centuries, many explorers and scientists believed the Arctic was just like Antarctica and was a thick layer of ice sitting on top of a vast continent. That was until 1958 when submariners (people who use submarines) sailed right under the Arctic ice cap and came out the other side, proving once and for all that the Arctic is just a giant piece of floating ice.

YOUNG SCIENTIST ACTIVITY
How to Airlift Ice

With this little experiment, you won't blow up the North Pole but you will be able to imagine what it might be like to airlift off the top of the planet. Using a little skill you will be able airlift ice out of a glass with just a piece of string and some very clever science.

EQUIPMENT NEEDED:

One glass

One piece of string around 6 inches (15 cm) long

One ice cube

Cold water

Salt

INSTRUCTIONS:

1. Take the empty glass and fill it with cold tap water.

2. Place the ice in the glass of water. Now place one end of the string on top of the ice cube with the other end hanging over the side of the glass.

3. Take the salt and sprinkle a small amount onto the ice cube and leave for 10–15 minutes.

4. After 10–15 minutes lift the string and see what happens.

Science Factoid

The string freezes to the ice cube, and when you pull on the string, it will lift the cube right out of the glass and into the air. This bonding happens when the salt and ice make contact. The salt lowers the freezing point of water slightly to just below 32° F (0° C). As a result, the ice cube partially melts but later refreezes and bonds the string to the ice cube.

Man Versus Nature

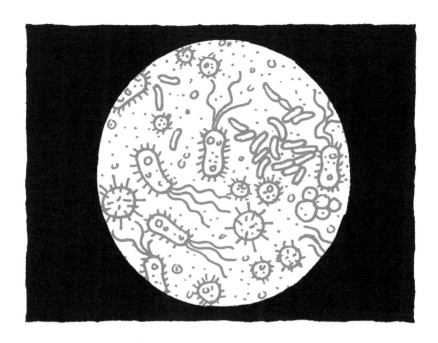

Deadly Diseases

In defense of human beings, they can't be blamed for inventing disease. It is, after all, the product of the biology of all living things, but unlike any other life-form humans have sought to mess with and rearrange almost every part of the planet. During this mixing, messing and meddling, humans have helped to create all manner of deadly disease that is then spread to other humans by touching, breathing, sneezing, open cuts and sores, insect bites or through contaminated foods and water.

Throughout history, humans have been wiped out by all sorts of "epidemics" and "pandemics." The first word is science speak for a disease that has spread and can be measured at country level or a region within that country. The second is science-speak for a disease that has reached international level and is spread across more than one country. Some of the deadliest diseases that threaten humans today follow.

TRYPANOSOMIASIS AKA SLEEPING SICKNESS

This disease is deadly but the early signs are quite ordinary, which makes it difficult to detect at first. You will feel a headache, begin to run a fever, may start vomiting and begin to have naps during the daytime, hence the name "sleeping sickness." Toward the end of the sickness, it gets really nasty, and sufferers often experience periods of madness before falling into a coma, then dying. Worse still, it can be a fairly slow process, taking up to three years for death to occur.

How do you get it?

The disease is caused by a little parasite in the blood that is spread by the bite of the tsetse fly.

MALARIA

Malaria is a very serious disease that can kill if not treated. If not handled properly, the symptoms of the disease can last many years and the sufferer feels tired all of the time and completely lacking in energy. Even today, the disease kills almost 2 million children each year in Africa.

How do you get it?

It is spread by an infectious parasitic protozoan that settles in your liver and attacks your red blood cells. Female mosquitoes spread it by carrying the protozoan from one victim to the next.

CHOLERA

This infection is characterized by violent vomiting and diarrhea. Historically, cholera was a major killer, but due to simple medical improvements, such as rehydration medicines and antibiotics, deaths have been greatly reduced.

How do you get it?

This is an easy one—Cholera is spread by drinking contaminated water, so if you're unsure don't drink it!

EBOLA VIRUS

This disease originated near the Ebola river in the Democratic Republic of the Congo and was recognized back in 1976. It is caused by a virus that attacks and completely breaks down your body tissue. This process has a pretty scary side effect that causes blood to flow from every opening in your body including your eyes, your ears, your nose and so on. Death is quick (a matter of days!) and around 90 percent of people infected die.

How do you get it?

The virus is spread in a number of ways, including eating infected monkey meat or by coming in contact with the blood or body fluids of an infected person.

PNEUMONIC PLAGUE

This one has been around for a very long time. It is an infection of the lungs that can be life-threatening and spreads rapidly as sufferers cough it out and make it airborne. The pneumonia progresses over 2 to 4 days and may cause septic shock and, without early treatment, death.

How do you get it?

Initially people thought it was spread by rats, but it was later discovered that the disease came from fleas that were carried by the rats and not the rats themselves.

TB, AKA TUBERCULOSIS

TB is a disease that attacks the lungs with over 3 million deaths each year. TB is a worldwide pandemic. Among the 15 countries with the highest estimated TB incidence rates, 13 are in Africa, while a third of all new cases are in India and China.

How do you get it?

TB can be spread by droplets of a cough from someone who is infected or even by drinking milk that is untreated from an infected animal.

Now You Sea Me, Now You Don't
(How to Make a Sea Vanish)

This is an experiment that humans didn't actually mean to go wrong, but stupidly they caused it to and made an entire sea vanish.

If you ever manage to visit the countries of Kazakhstan and Uzbekistan, which are to the south of Russia, you will be forgiven for not believing your eyes. As you stand on the dusty sea bed of what used to be the Aral Sea, you will witness the strange site of camels crossing the sands passing by dozens and dozens of enormous fishing boats just stranded on a dry, dusty desert known as a "ship graveyard."

Once upon a time, the Aral Sea was the world's fourth-largest inland sea, but in the past 50 years it has shrunk to just 10 percent of its original size due to incredibly bad management by humans. The sea, which borders Uzbekistan and Kazakhstan and was once 26,000 square miles (67,000 km^2, that's about half the size of England) has dried up because since the 1960s the rivers that fed the sea were diverted 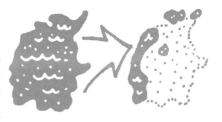 or redirected by the Russian government in an attempt to increase cotton production in the area. This meant that by 2007 the sea had been reduced to just a tenth of its original size and began to split into separate areas of water.

The disaster has ruined the fishing industry of the area and has left fishing trawlers stranded in sandy deserts as if they had been dropped there without any reason. The former fishing town of Muynak in Uzbekistan has a large pier that simply stretches out into the desert.

What little water is left is of little use to local people as it has been heavily polluted by the pesticides and fertilizers that run off the farmland and into the remaining water supply—a situation that has created severe pollution and major health problems for local people.

In recent years, attempts have been made to clean up the waterways and try to grow the sea again, but with much division between countries and a serious lack of cooperation, the poor Aral Sea appears doomed for the history books, another clear example of humans messing up the planet.

HOW TO MAKE YOUR VERY OWN SEA VANISH

1. Take a large, salty water body.

2. Cut off all its supply chains for water such as rivers and streams.

3. Wait a very long time—remember, it took over 50 years to dry up the Aral Sea.

4. Add fertilizers and pesticides to the water to finally kill it off and make the water unusable.

5. Stand back and admire your handiwork—you should now have a moon-like scene of dry desert, no water and fleets upon fleets of boats and fishing trawlers stranded where your sea used to be. Well done—"sea" you later!

YOUNG SCIENTIST ACTIVITY
Disappearing Messages

Just like the Aral Sea, this activity will show you how to write secret messages that also disappear right in front of your eyes.

EQUIPMENT NEEDED:

One bowl

One lemon

One spoon

Sheets of paper

Water

One cotton swab

One light

INSTRUCTIONS:

1. Cut your lemon in half and squeeze both ends into the bowl.

2. Add just a few drops of water to the lemon juice and stir with your spoon.

3. Take the cotton bud and dip it into the water/lemon mix.

4. Use the cotton swab on one of the sheets of paper to write a secret message.

5. As the message dries, it will disappear.

6. To read it, hold the sheet in front of a lit lightbulb.

Science Factoid

The secret to the science in this experiment is held inside the lemon. Lemons and other fruits contain carbon. In water, carbon is practically colorless, which makes your message almost impossible to see. However, when carbon is exposed to heat it decays and turns black. That is what happens when the paper is held close to the lightbulb, making your secret message visible.

Attack of the Blob! —Seriously Slimy Sea Snot

You may have thought that snot and boogers were just the gooey green stuff that shot out of your nose when you sneezed, but what if you discovered snot on a much bigger and gooier scale? In recent years, scientists are discovering more and more outbreaks of the mucus-like material in our oceans, which they have nicknamed "sea snot," and they believe that these enormous areas of oozing unpleasantness are on the increase due to warmer sea temperatures caused by global warming.

Areas of sea snot can grow as big as 120 miles long (200 km) and seem to appear naturally. They are most common during the summer months near the Mediterranean coast. Scientists think warm weather makes the seawater more stable, which sets up the ideal conditions for the bonding of the organic matter that makes up the giant gooey blobs. What's worse is the fact that scientists say that warming temperatures are helping the stuff form even in the winter months.

IS THIS GOO NEW?

Not really, newspapers from as far back as the 1800s reported stories of people at the beach holding their noses when a piece of stinky sea snot ran aground, but until recently it was only seen as an inconvenience that left swimmers covered in goo and fishing nets clogged up with the stuff. Now scientists have discovered that the snot could be deadly, containing viruses and bacteria such as E. coli. This toxic stuff is a major threat to the health of swimmers and all marine creatures.

WHERE IS THE SCUM FROM?

Sea snot starts out life as a whole bunch of tiny living and dead organic matter scientists call "marine snow." It then begins to snowball and grow in size picking up more and more matter. The blobs then become perfect hosts for viruses and bacteria. Many coastal communities affected by the goo have to regularly test for E. coli because its presence has been enough to close beaches to swimmers.

WHAT CAN THE GOO DO TO YOU?

- Doctors report that swimmers who pass through the goo can often develop nasty skin conditions like dermatitis, which can make skin red, sore and cracked.

- Fish and other sea-based animals that swim in the goo are most greatly exposed to bacteria, which often kills them.

- The larger blobs can even trap animals by coating their gills in the thick substance and suffocating them, which could reduce our marine food supplies.

YOUNG SCIENTIST ACTIVITY
Make Your Own Slimy Sea Snot

Although it might seem disgusting, this activity will help you make a squishy mess that you can twist, shape and stretch.

EQUIPMENT NEEDED:

Water

Green food coloring

One large mixing bowl

One cereal bowl

PVA glue

Borax

A cup

A tablespoon

INSTRUCTIONS:

1. Take the large mixing bowl and cover the bottom of it with the PVA glue.

2. Then add in several tablespoons of water and stir together.

3. Now add in two or three drops of food coloring and stir again.

4. Fill up the cup with water and add one tablespoon of Borax and mix. Add this solution into the large mixing bowl.

5. Finally, stir it all together and move it all to the cereal bowl. Shortly, the mixture will begin to act just like slimy, stinky sea snot.

Science Factoid

The Borax contains a chemical named sodium borate, while the glue is what scientists call a "polymer." When both meet in the water solution, they join together into one large molecule. The new material can absorb water really easily to give a gooey, squishy substance that acts just like sea snot. The green color just adds to the effect!

ALIENS! *A CAST OF THOUSANDS!*

Alien versus Predator

An "alien" species is not from another planet but is the scientific name given to a plant or animal from a different area or ecosystem. Due to worldwide trade and travel, humans have badly messed up many of our ecosystems by bringing many alien species of plants and animals into places where they don't belong and it has at times had devastating effects. Remember, before humans began to explore other continents, ecosystems remained fairly separate and over millions of years the native plants and animals evolved in isolation from one another. Today, however, the influence of humans has really thrown a wrench in the works and have either purposely or accidentally mixed species from one ecosystem with species from another. Let's take a closer look.

WHO'S THE DADDY?

This story is the tale of what happens when you take the top predator from one ecosystem and let it run into the top predator from another ecosystem. Before you read on, I need to tell you that it isn't going to look good.

The giant Burmese python is an enormous snake from Burma in Southeast Asia, but in the U.S. you don't even have to catch a plane flight to find one because you only have to travel to the state of Florida. Down in the Everglades, you'll find lots of pythons which have either escaped or simply been released into the waters by careless owners because they've grown too big for their tanks. Don't forget that these babies can grow to more than 20 feet (6 m) and are capable of swallowing a full-grown goat. What happens when one animal at the top of the food chain meets its opposite number? In October 2005, evidence of one such struggle turned up when researchers found a dead, headless python after it tried to eat a 6-foot-long (2 m) alligator. The alligator was found poking out of a hole in the middle of the python with chunks of the alligator's skin later found inside the python.

Experts are unsure how this battle panned out. Some believe the alligator must have been ill or wounded to have been swallowed. Others believe the python could have won but bit off more than it could chew and burst open. Battles between alligators and pythons have been rising in the Everglades for the last 20 years as the Asian invader has thrived in the alligator's own backyard.

MORE MIX-UPS

The same craziness is taking place all over the planet. In almost every region and ecosystem, animals and plants that evolved separately are appearing where they're not wanted and humans are to blame. Here are just a handful of alien species.

- The cane toad, which originates in the Americas, was introduced to northern Queensland, Australia over 75 years ago as a means to control the damaging sugarcane beetles, but the humans hadn't really thought it through. You see, cane toads carry a poison on their backs that is deadly to Australia's predators like dingoes and even crocodiles. When threatened, they will secrete their deadly venom, which can cause rapid heartbeats, excessive salivation, convulsions and paralysis. As a result, the predators leave the cane toads to their own devices, and they now number into the billions and are spreading right across Australia at an alarming rate.

- The tiny Caribbean coqui tree frog may look cute but the little invader to Hawaii is hated by the people of the islands because of its constant and deafening croak, which can hit the level of 90 decibels—a noise louder than a car alarm or garden mower, and if you have a whole bunch of them in your backyard . . . well, you can kiss a good night's sleep good-bye.

- Just after World War II, the brown tree snake from Australia and New Guinea was accidently transported in a bunch of military equipment and was delivered to the island of Guam. The tree snake had no predator and lots of food supply (perfect!). The snakes boomed over time and reached densities of almost 13,000 per square mile (2.6 km²). In the meantime, the reptile has been so damaging, eight of the island's eleven native bird species are now gone.

FANCY FENCES

- In some parts of the world, alien invaders have been so devastating that governments have had to take drastic measure to control populations. In Australia, they have built fences to control the explosion of rabbits introduced in the nineteenth century from Europe. Our floppy-eared friend has caused millions of dollars of damage to the environment. In 1907, the rabbit-proof fences were first built in western Australia in an attempt to contain the rabbits. They now total a distance of 2,021 miles (3,253 km) but even this hasn't been a full success because as the bodies of dead rabbits piled up along the fence, they formed a ramp for those still living to jump across to new pastures.

- Likewise, as three species of Asian carp escaped from catfish farms into the Mississippi River, the U.S. and state governments had to invest in a $10 million electrified barrier to keep the carp out of the Great Lakes by shooting electrical pulses out to make the carp turn around and leave the lakes.

Towers of Silence . . . Silenced

In India in the early 1990s, humans managed to single-handedly take one species of bird to the brink of extinction. The vulture may not be the most appealing animal to look at, and when you find out what they feed on, you may be turned off from our feathered friend even more and may need to barf. You see, vultures feed on dead and decomposing animals . . . basically rotting flesh, which might sound disgusting, but vultures perform a vital job for our ecosystems—they break down and recycle dead matter very quickly. Without them, things would be much more stomach-churning and rather smelly.

MESSING WITH NATURE

So, what happens when humans mess with an ecosystem? Well humans nearly pushed vultures in India to the point of extinction at a scarily rapid rate. Some say they declined faster than the now-extinct dodo's disappearance. In less than 15 years, vulture numbers fell as much as 97 percent in India alone. This created massive unforeseen problems, including large numbers of rotting cattle carcasses in the streets of Bombay and huge packs of wild dogs feasting on the remains. Matters were only made worse by the fact that most of the wild dogs were infected with rabies—a disease that drives infected people insane before most of its victims die.

Even with all this chaos and disease, the Indian government would not permit scientists to examine the vultures to get to the bottom of their massive decline, and this negatively affected one group of people in India—the Parsis.

The Parsis are a very traditional group who practice one of the least polluting and most ecologically sound religions on Earth. Their religion follows a 3,000-year-old belief that you must not cremate, bury or submerge the dead because they see the corpses as impure and they do not want these impurities to infect the natural systems of this planet. They see the five elements of fire, air, water, soil and sky as sacred. Instead, the dead must be left on hilltops for vultures that come to feed in the Towers of Silence in Bombay. It is common for Parsis to travel long distances to take their dead to the towers, as prayers for the dead can only be said for those who have passed through its gates. But with vulture numbers falling to just 3 percent of their original number, many Parsi corpses were left to rot and pollute the air and water. Over a matter of weeks, bodies began to pile up at the towers—a situation that caused terrible distress to the Parsi people and the residents of Bombay. Fortunately, the scientists were eventually allowed to look at the dead vultures to get to the root of their virtual extinction. Autopsies showed that they had suffered from kidney failure caused by the use of a cheap anti-inflammatory drug used on cattle, which was deadly to the vultures. So, if you ever feel disgusted by wiggling maggots, flies or even vultures . . . remember, without these guys we'd be in a whole other pile of mess.

TRIVIA MARVELOUS MAGGOTS

You may be surprised, but there have been many uses for maggots throughout history. They have long been used to remove dead or damaged tissue from humans by the medical industry. The maggots feed only on the dead tissue and leave the live tissue unharmed. This process is referred to as "maggot therapy," and it is still used today in some places.

Maggots are also used in the forensic science industry, with police and scientists using them to help solve cases by dating corpses and determining time of death.

Faking the Planet

Humans have become so expert at messing with the planet that they can now actually "fake" some of it. Yes, we can now recreate parts of the planet and make it look like they were there naturally. We have fake beaches, fake islands and even fake countries.

LIFE'S A BEACH . . . JUST NOT A REAL ONE

Pretty much every beach is built in a very normal and straightforward process—the inward rush of a wave onto the shore is called the "swash." It carries sand, gravel and pebbles on to the beach. As the wave retreats back down the beach, the backwash carries sand and gravel out to sea. Since waves normally hit the beach at an angle, but always go straight out, the waves gradually move sand and gravel along the beach in a zigzagging process known as "longshore drift." When the swash is stronger than the backwash, then a large beach will build up, but when the reverse is true, nature will quickly "eat" into a beach and eventually make it disappear. All okay with that then? Not really, because as you well know humans don't really like nature because it messes with human plans and gets in the way. Take Miami Beach in the U.S. for instance—it started out fine and was a very successful beach. It attracted loads of tourists, and, as a result, hotels, casinos, restaurants and other tourist facilities sprouted up along the beachfront, but then longshore drift started to eat away at the beach and it began to disappear. This created great alarm, after all, why visit a beach with no beach?

Humans began to rebuild the beach in a process called "beach nourishment." Today those who visit Miami Beach can sunbathe on a beach that has been carried up the coast in the back of a truck and dumped there to create a fake beach. The process is repeated every five years or so to replace the sand that the waves continually take away.

THE FAKE ISLANDS

Humans don't just stop at the odd beach or two. No! they can make their very own islands from scratch, as well. The Palm Islands in Dubai are three giant man-made islands in the shape of palm trees, each surrounded by a crescent island. The islands, named Palm Jumeirah, Palm Jebel Ali and Palm Deira are home to expensive hotels, apartments as well as restaurants, shops and leisure facilities. The Palm Islands will add 323 miles (520 km) of fake beachfront to the city of Dubai.

LET'S FAKE A COUNTRY

Even though the country of the Netherlands juts out into the North Atlantic Ocean, for hundreds of years the Dutch people have been pushing away the ocean. In an attempt to create more land for farming and living, the people of the Netherlands began to build dikes to keep the sea out and used wind pumps to drain this new land dry starting way back around 1200 AD. Now more than 60 percent of the population of the Netherlands lives below sea level on this piece of reclaimed, fake land. With rising sea levels, the country is in a very tricky situation and if the dikes were to give way, there would be a lot of people in great danger.

REDRAW THE WHOLE PLANET

On the topic of global warming and sea-level rise, some scientists believe that sea-level rise from the melting ice caps will be so bad that the entire world map will need to be redrawn as the shape of countries all over the planet changes due to flooding.

In some areas, such as low-lying islands in the Pacific, a three-foot (1 m) rise in sea levels will be disastrous and they would disappear off the map completely. Florida's Everglades could be completely submerged, and parts of Manhattan would be swallowed by the sea.

YOUNG SCIENTIST ACTIVITY
The (Fake) Leaky Bottle

This activity is a bit of a fake and will completely confuse you. If you get it right, it won't make any sense at all.

EQUIPMENT NEEDED:

One set of pliers

One nail

Water

One plastic bottle with a screw cap

INSTRUCTIONS:

1. Take the plastic bottle and make around 10–12 holes in the base of the bottle using the nail. Do this by holding the nail with the pliers and pushing hard through the plastic.

2. Once you have made the holes, set the bottle in the kitchen sink with the plughole plugged.

3. Now run two inches (5 cm) of water so that the water level is above the level of the bottom of the bottle. You will have to use your other hand to hold the bottle steady in the water.

4. While still keeping the bottle in the water, slide it beneath the tap and fill it completely.

5. Lift the bottle above the water level for a second or two to make sure water drips out of the bottom.

6. Place it back in the water and fill up any water lost and screw the cap back on the bottle before slowly lifting it out of the water again. The results will appear quite strange.

Science Factoid

A few drips of water may form around the holes but the bottle refuses to leak. You can then remove the cap and watch the water drip out. Outside air pressure is holding the water inside the bottle, creating a situation that appears completely fake—a leaky bottle that doesn't leak. When the cap is removed, the same air pressure pushes down through the mouth of the bottle and forces the water out.

Dumbest Ideas Ever

In this chapter we are going to look at some of the dumbest ideas that the scientists of this world came up with, but thankfully never really took off!

PROJECT PIGEON

Back in 1941, an American scientist called B. F. Skinner felt pigeons were the answer to defeating Adolf Hitler in World War II. Skinner proved that our little feathered friends could steer a missile toward a model ship by simply pecking at a target on a screen, which then moved the rudders on the missile. Skinner's pigeons would continue to peck with incredible accuracy even in the last few seconds of rapid descent and with explosions going off all around them. Skinner intended to load three pigeons inside each missile cone, but plans for pigeon piloted bombs were eventually cancelled in 1944 because government officials just couldn't trust pigeons to fly and control such dangerous weapons.

AN INDOOR BIG APPLE

In the 1950s, inventor Richard Buckminster Fuller designed a giant dome to cover two miles (3.2 km) of sky above New York. He felt his idea would stop the streets of Manhattan from being blocked by snow during New York's harsh winters. Fuller planned for the "roof" to be pulled into place using 16 enormous helicopters, creating a little indoor city. Unfortunately, New Yorkers could not be convinced that it was good value for money to pay $200 million to stay indoors all day so the idea was canned.

THE ESCAPE COFFIN

Just in case a dead body decided it wasn't too keen on death anymore, in 1868 Franz Vester invented the escape coffin. This burial box came complete with an escape ladder and a pull cord that would ring a bell around the local graveyard where the body was buried. It has never been manufactured.

THE ALL-NEW NUCLEAR CAR

The Ford Nucleon was to be the world's first-ever nuclear-powered car and at first the idea looked good. Fuel economy, for instance, was incredible with a promised 5,000 miles (8,000 km) of travel without needing to refuel. In 1958, scientists were convinced that atomic-powered automobiles with their own onboard nuclear reactors would be a brilliant transport solution that would revolutionize the global automobile market. Importantly, it was realized that even the smallest of car accidents could result in an entire city getting nuked so the brilliant plan was dropped.

The "Grim Reaper" Scale

S cientists have always drawn up scales to measure and compare the size of things. Take the "F" scale, for instance, used to measure the strength of tornado winds, or the Richter scale, which grades the size of earthquakes. But there is one scientific scale that is weirder and creepier than any other scale on Earth. The Duckworth Scale, named after its inventor, Dr. Frank Duckworth, is also jokingly referred to as "the Grim Reaper scale" because of the strange things it attempts to measure.

You see, the Duckworth Scale measures the likelihood or chance of a person dying as a result of carrying out any given activity.

The scale runs from 0 to 8, with 0 being the safest kind of activity you could be involved in and 8 being one that will result in certain death.

Dr. Duckworth has graded a whole range of human activities from washing up to flying on a plane, and you might just be surprised at some of the results. For example, if you are a 35-year-old male who smokes 40 cigarettes then you will be very high on the scale with a score of 7.1—a score which is, amazingly, almost as dangerous as playing Russian roulette with a single bullet loaded in the gun (scoring 7.2).

The table below shows the Duckworth Scale and the increasing chances of death from various activities as the number on the scale increases.

LEVEL ON SCALE	HUMAN ACTIVITY
0.0	Complete safety (living on Earth unharmed for a year)
0.3	Single 100-mile (160 km) rail journey
1.6	Being hit by an asteroid (in the lifetime of a newborn male)
1.7	Single 100-mile (160 km) flight
1.9	Single 100-mile (160 km) car journey (by sober middle-aged male)
4.2	Rock climbing (single session)
4.6	Murder (in the lifetime of a newborn male)
5.5	Vacuuming; washing up; walking down the street; car accident (in the lifetime of a newborn male); accidental fall (newborn baby boy)

6.3	Rock climbing (for over 20 years)
6.4	Deep-sea fishing (for over 40 years)
7.1	Smoking (35-year-old male, 40 a day)
7.2	Russian roulette (single game, one bullet)
8.0	Russian roulette (single game, six bullets); jumping off the Eiffel Tower; lying down in front of a speeding train

Who'd have thought a single 100-mile (160 km) car journey driven by a middle-aged man would be more life-threatening than being killed by an asteroid?

TRIVIA   In reality, the Duckworth scale is incredibly accurate and it is highly unlikely that you will be hit by an asteroid, despite the image presented by moviemakers and the media. What is even more interesting is the naming process associated with newly discovered asteroids. The IAU (International Astronomical Union) has its own committee for naming asteroids, and it is safe to say that they have come up with some beauties. Some of the most famous bodies of rock flying above our heads include Humptydumpty, Hippo, Bus, Lick, Mr. Spock, Fanny, Janeausten and Robinhood to name just a few!

RESOURCES

Websites to Check Out

Amusement Park Physics: www.learner.org/interactives/parkphysics/index.html. Interactive website about the science behind park rides.

Bill Nye the Science Guy: www.billnye.com. Fun facts can be found in episode guides, and the website also has fun videos and experiments.

Brain Pop: www.brainpop.com/free_stuff. Animated videos and quizzes about science, health, technology and more.

Cool Science for Curious Kids: www.hhmi.org/coolscience/forkids. Interactive articles and experiments on biology questions.

Defenders of Wildlife: www.defenders.org. Wildlife and environment news and animal fact sheets.

Discovery Kids: kids.discovery.com. Articles, activities, and games about science, crafts and more.

Earth Rangers: www.earthrangers.com. Videos, games and blog about endangered animals and how to help them.

Exploratorium museum in San Francisco: www.exploratorium.edu. Lots of interactive information, videos, and things to try on your own.

Extreme Science: www.extremescience.com. Articles about the science behind the biggest, baddest, and the best of several types of animals and other natural phenomena.

Funology: www.funology.com. Games and jokes, but also trivia, experiments, and hands-on activities.

The Greens: www.meetthegreens.org. Animated videos, blog and games on eco-conscious living.

How Stuff Works: www.howstuffworks.com. Lots of articles and videos on a wide variety of subjects.

National Geographic Kids: kids.nationalgeographic.com. News, photos, videos, experiments and games on many topics.

Ocean Explorer by NOAA: oceanexplorer.noaa.gov. Articles on current and historical exploration expeditions in the ocean. Also photos and videos of ocean plant and animal life.

Popular Science: www.popsci.com. Articles and videos about current science and technology.

Science Made Simple: www.sciencemadesimple.com. Science fair project ideas, articles and experiments.

ScienceMonster.com. Fun articles in a variety of science topics and online games.

Science News for Kids: www.sciencenewsforkids.org. Intriguing articles and photos in several categories of science.

Sea and Sky: www.seasky.org. Interactive articles and online games about oceanography and astronomy.

Strange Science: www.strangescience.net. Photos and information on the history of paleontology and the mistakes made as scientists began learning about strange creatures.

TryScience: tryscience.com. An interactive website full of experiments to do online and at home.

Tunza, United Nations Environment Programme: www.unep.org/Tunza. News, stories of kids making a difference and listings of activities and conferences around the world.

Books to Read

NONFICTION AND ACTIVITIES

Becklake, Sue. *The Visual Dictionary of the Universe.* Eyewitness Visual Dictionaries, DK Publishing, 1993.

Berkenkamp, Lauri. *Kid Disasters and How to Fix Them.* Norwich, Vermont: Nomad Press, 2002.

Blakey, Nancy. *Go Outside!* Berkeley, California: Tricycle Press, 2002.

Branzei, Sylvia. *Animal Grossology.* New York: Price Stern Sloan, 2004.

———. *Grossology.* New York: Price Stern Sloan, 2002.

———. *Grossology and You.* New York: Price Stern Sloan, 2002.

———. *Hands-On Grossology.* New York: Price Stern Sloan, 2003.

Cobb, Vicki. *Magic . . . Naturally! Science Entertainments & Amusements.* New York: T. B. Lippincott, 1976.

———. *You Gotta Try This! Absolutely Irresistible Science.* New York: Morrow Junior Books, 1999.

———, and Kathy Darling. *Wanna Bet? Science Challenges to Fool You.* New York: Lothrop, Lee & Shepard Books, 1993.

Elsaeed, Rasha, and Chris Oxlade, editors. *150 Great Science Experiments.* New York: Lorenz Books, 2001.

Facklam, Margery. *What Does the Crow Know? The Mysteries of Animal Intelligence.* San Francisco: Sierra Club Books for Children, 1994.

Ficarra, John, and Nick Megline, eds. *The Mad Gross Book.* New York: MAD Books, 2001.

Friedhoffer, Bob. *Magic and Perception: The Art and Science of Fooling the Senses.* New York: Franklin Watts, 1996.

Goodman, Susan E. *The Truth about Poop.* London: Puffin Books, 2007.

Green, Joey. *Paint Your House with Powdered Milk.* New York: Hyperion, 1996.

———. *The Mad Scientist Handbook: The Do-It-Yourself Guide to Making Your Own Rock Candy, Anti-Gravity Machine, Edible Glass, Rubber Eggs, Fake Blood, Green Slime, and Much Much More.* New York: Perigee Books, 2000.

Guinness World Records, 2013. New York: Guinness World Records, 2012.

Gurstelle, William. *Backyard Ballistics.* Chicago: Chicago Review Press, 2001.

King, Bart. *The Big Book of Boy Stuff.* Salt Lake City: Gibbs Smith, 2004.

———. *The Big Book of Girl Stuff.* Salt Lake City: Gibbs Smith, 2006.

———. *The Big Book of Gross Stuff.* Salt Lake City: Gibbs Smith, 2010.

———. *The Pocket Guide to Games.* Salt Lake City: Gibbs Smith, 2008.

Lee, Fran. *Wishing on a Star: Constellation Stories and Stargazing Activities for Kids.* Salt Lake City: Gibbs Smith, 2001.

Masoff, Joy. *Oh, Yikes! History's Grossest Moments.* New York: Workman Publishing, 2006.

———. *Oh, Yuck! The Encyclopedia of Everything Nasty.* New York: Workman Publishing, 2000.

McManners, Hugh. *The Outdoor Adventure Handbook.* New York: Dorling Kindersley Publishing, 1996.

Panati, Charles. *Panati's Extraordinary Origins of Everyday Things.* New York: Perennial Library, 1987.

Piven, Joshua. *The Worst-Case Scenario Survival Handbook.* San Francisco: Chronicle Books, 1999.

Rauzon, Mark J. and Cynthia Overbeck Bix. *Water, Water Everywhere.* San Francisco: Sierra Club Books for Children, 1995.

Ryder, Joanne. *The Waterfall's Gift.* San Francisco: Sierra Club Books for Children, 2001.

Sabatino, Chris. *Monster Doodles for Kids.* Salt Lake City: Gibbs Smith, 2011.

———. *Dinosaur Doodles for Kids.* Salt Lake City: Gibbs Smith, 2012.

Solheim, James. *It's Disgusting—and We Ate It! True Food Facts from Around the World—and Throughout History!* New York: Simon and Schuster Books for Young Readers, 1998.

Spignesi, Stephen J. *The 100 Greatest Disasters of All Time.* Sacramento, California: Citadel Press, 2002.

Taylor, Barbara. *How to Save the Planet.* New York: Franklin Watts, 2001.

Williams, Zac. *Little Monsters Cookbook.* Salt Lake City: Gibbs Smith, 2010.

FICTION

Adams, Douglas. *The Hitchhiker's Guide to the Galaxy.* New York: Ballantine, 1997.

Burroughs, Edgar Rice. *Tarzan of the Apes.* New York: Ballantine Books, 1990. (Check out his other books, too.)

Johnston, Tony. *Isabel's House of Butterflies.* San Francisco: Sierra Club Books for Children, 2003.

Lewis, C. S. *The Lion, the Witch, and the Wardrobe.* New York: HarperCollins, 1994. (Read the rest of the Narnia series when you finish this one.)

Philbrick, Rodman. *Freak the Mighty.* New York: Scholastic, 2001.

Rockwell, Thomas. *How to Eat Fried Worms.* New York: F. Watts, 1973.

Rowling, J. K. *Harry Potter and the Sorcerer's Stone, Harry Potter and the Chamber of Secrets, Harry Potter and the Prisoner of Azkaban, Harry Potter and the Goblet of Fire, Harry Potter and the Order of the Phoenix, Harry Potter and the Half-Blood Prince* and *Harry Potter and the Deathly Hallows.* (New York: Arthur A. Levine Books, 1998–2007).

Sachar, Louis. *Holes.* New York: Yearling Books, 2000.

———. *Sideways Stories from Wayside School.* New York: HarperCollins, 1978.

———. *There's a Boy in the Girl's Bathroom.* New York: Yearling Books, 1987.

Salisbury, Graham. *Under the Blood Red Sun.* New York: Delacorte Press, 1994.

———. *Shark Bait.* New York: Delacorte Press, 1997.

Schwartz, Alvin. *Scary Stories to Tell in the Dark.* New York: HarperCollins, 1981.

Scieszka, Jon. *Knights of the Kitchen Table.* New York: Puffin Books, 1994.

Shan, Darren. Vampire series that begins with *Cirque du Freak.* Boston: Little, Brown, 2001.

Stine, R. L. *Welcome to Dead House.* New York: Scholastic, 1992. (This is the first book in the "Goosebumps" series. Try it, read more in the series or check out his other books.)

Tolkien, J. R. R. *The Hobbit, The Fellowship of the Ring, The Two Towers* and *The Return of the King.* (New York: Del Rey Books, 2012.)

Yep, Laurence. *Dragonwings.* New York: HarperCollins, 1987.

Zelazny, Roger. A great writer. Try *Roadmarks* or *Unicorn Variations* (New York: Avon, 1987) for starters.

Check out more science fun with James Doyle's
A Young Scientist's Guide to Defying Disasters

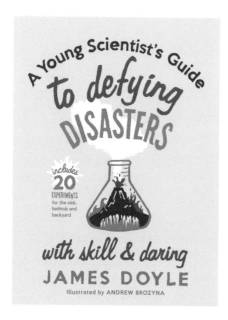

160 pages, $14.99
Available at bookstores
or directly from Gibbs Smith
1.800.835.4993
www.gibbs-smith.com

Do you have a thirst for adventure and dodging danger?

If so, you are part of a very elite and specialized group of explorers who, by the end of this book, will have the firsthand skills and know-how to defy even the most dangerous situations on Earth.

Complete with hands-on experiments, *A Young Scientist's Guide to Defying Disasters* is your guide to surviving anything planet Earth can throw at you! Ever conquered a limnic eruption or a lahar? No? Well, kit up, engage your brain and prepare yourself for the ride of a lifetime.